Roughing the Pastor

A Pastor's Personal Experience in Surviving the Church

By "Rev"

With "Marge"

ISBN: 978-1-4269-8969-8 (sc)
ISBN: 978-1-4269-8970-4 (e)

Trafford rev. 08/09/2011

 www.trafford.com

North America & international
toll-free: 1 888 232 4444 (USA & Canada)
phone: 250 383 6864 ♦ fax: 812 355 4082

Table of Contents

CHAPTER 1:

What Have I Gotten Into?

I cannot say what conceptions other men and women have who enter ministry, but I suspect few of us pastors expect to always be "at the top of our game" in totally trouble-free congregations. After all, if the world were perfect, we would not have a job. There would be no need for Truth proclaimed in pulpits.

For the sake of expediency, when referring to pastors, I will use the masculine pronoun, knowing we are all capable of expanding the pronoun to include both sexes who serve in ministry.

I do not believe I went into pastoral ministry naively. I did not think I would always have every member's loyalty and support, that my congregations would grow beyond even my superintendent's wildest imagination, or that people would be waiting at the church doors on Sunday mornings, hoping to beat others to get a front row seat to hear my remarkable sermons.

No, I went into the pastorate in response to what I believed was God's call upon my life, and though I did not doubt that God could do wonderful things through me, I knew it would take many acts of God to make me into a "real pastor". I sincerely wanted to become the best pastor I could become. I knew I needed God's grace and patience. I knew I also needed my congregations to be gracious and patient as I sought to present God's truths to them in all their circumstances.

I even expected to be humbled, and I did not fear that humbling, for humility is part of the process of becoming increasingly useful to God.

Because I did not intend to enter the ministry half-heartedly, I endeavored to become as fully "prepared" as one can, humanly speaking. I followed the training prescribed by my denomination.

But with my limited understanding, I reached times in my ministry when, in darkness and deep despair, I concluded that nothing, not even God, had prepared me for some of the behaviors of people who sat in my pews. In my ministry, I encountered people who knowingly, or unknowingly, worked to destroy any hope I had of fulfilling my pastoral calling. Seldom was the destruction I experienced apparent to others who had called me to serve them.

My pastoral experiences, though uniquely mine, are similar to experiences my fellow pastors have. By retelling experiences that derailed my ministry and mental health, and by citing behavior that led to my depression, which, in turn, left me less capable of fulfilling my vision as a pastor, I hope to help those within the congregation see how easily they can hinder, or help, a local church's God-given responsibility for a body of believers.

I fear that if congregational behavior within the body of Christ is not addressed, Christ's commission to the pastors and to the believers in any age will soon fail to be proclaimed because increasingly fewer will be willing to endure mental and emotional abuse inflicted upon those who answer the call to ministry. Of course, the result will then be that countless souls will unnecessarily spend eternity apart from God.

I write this "epistle" to you who sit in the pews to simply tell you that your Christian maturity often depends as much upon your pastor hearing kind, encouraging words from you and others sitting next to you as it does upon your pastor's hearing from God. Consequently,

I believe the maturity your pastor encourages and sees in you can indirectly further the effectiveness of his ministry to others.

My desire is to give you a clearer understanding of how one person's treatment of another person affects that person. That effect, I believe, is even more hurtful when it is treatment of a pastor. As painful as mistreatment is for all people it is especially painful to one who has poured out his soul while giving spiritual ministry to those very same people.

Am I saying a pastor is above reproach, that he is God's sinless appointment over you?

Not at all. If your pastor is not teaching Biblical truths, that is the time to find another pastor after following the steps of Mathew 18:15-20. What I am saying is simply that we pastors are sinners saved by grace. We are humans with emotions that sometimes do get away from the control of the Holy Spirit. Our perfection, like yours, will come after we join the sanctified believers around the throne in Heaven. We need parishioners to know that because of our humanness, unkind words we heard and cruel actions toward us pastors were often timed by the devil to happen when we are weak and vulnerable. Consequently, we pastors are sometimes rendered helpless, unable to carry on our ministry for a period of time or even for all of the earthly life that remains. Sometimes the congregational abuse leaves us with wounds so deep that the thought of continuing ministry, even continuing to live, seems pointless. I will admit that some abuse by those I came to serve sometimes cut me so deeply that I struggled with the temptation to respond in unspeakably sinful ways. By the grace of God, I did not act outwardly, but I let the abuse settle deep within to fester and poison me for decades.

Do I sound like I have an ax to grind? Well, in fact, I do, but not just because I alone had some despicable experiences. I have heard from many pastors who have that same ax to grind.

Because I have lived with the memories of pastoral abuse long enough I am compelled to speak out. What happened to me in the churches I served years ago cannot change, but I hope my words will help prevent further attempts, intentional or otherwise, from occurring within the body of Christ.

Since retirement, my social life has been more like the life of a layman than like a pastor. This change has given me a good look at both sides of this issue. I am deeply disturbed whenever I hear a pastor criticized.

I do not wish to come across as a complainer, but lack of respect for pastors is a serious matter. From conversations with other pastors and observations I've made since leaving the ministry early, I can say with certainty that abuse of pastors and their families has not yet ended. Praise God for congregations who intentionally speak words and do things that will graciously benefit a pastor's ministry and actively prevent abuse of the minister and his family.

There are, however, some wolves in sheep's clothing, maybe even in your church.

To you who act as if you have a Divine call to keep your pastor humble, and there seems to be at least one in every church, and to you who just throw out a negative remark now and then, take heed. Even one negative remark has a serious effect on your pastor and on you, yes you, and on others. Your negativity spreads like wildfire. Some will even pick up your words and add, "Now that you mentioned that, I think of the time when..."

Yes, I do have an ax to grind. Memories of the treatment I received during my ministry continued to haunt me. My emotional well-being crumbled. I have lived with that for years and would continue so except for the Lord ministering to me through His Holy Word and through others in human flesh. Writing this book, as much as the memories have hurt, has also helped me to let go of much of the past. During my years of depression Bible reading had suffered greatly. I had to get back to it, and even that was an effort. It became more like a chore that had to be done. I am still seeking and praying for a deeper love for The Holy Scriptures. Retirement, with all those awful memories weighing heavy on the heart and mind, has not been the joy that retirement ought to be.

Yes, I have an ax to grind, and it is not *my* ax only. When the situation came to a head in Church "G", of which you will read in the pages that follow, the word got around. My goodness how quickly the news of a pastor having trouble in his church travels! I guess people like to talk about such things. Soon I was getting phone calls from other pastors going through similar difficulties. Mostly they just wanted to let loose and talk to someone who would understand, but they also wanted to know if I had a word that could help them in their situations. How can a lame man help another lame man walk?

One of the callers was a young pastor who told of his seminary classmates who had returned to the classroom after their year of internship. As they were sharing their experiences, those soon-to-be-pastors realized that each one of them had been wounded during that first year in the field.

I recall that among my own classmates returning from internship, there were those who decided they wanted no more of the treatment they received during their internship and did not return to seminary. They had previously testified of God's call to ministry, but now another power had dominated.

One member of my seminary class did not get a good report from his internship church. Probably for that reason, two years later when he had completed seminary studies, he could not get a call to a church. He transferred to another denomination. He and I served internship churches that were only about 20 minutes apart. We got together often during that time. I know he had a good ministry, but there was a strong, domineering leader in that church who was very critical of the pastor. The bad report that was sent to the seminary office came from the critic. One person can ruin a pastor's ministry.

Remember, friends, these seminarians had been certain of God's call to ministry, but someone in their first congregation set up a roadblock that became, or looked like, too much of a hurdle to make it possible to follow that call. Yes, God is Sovereign, but I ask you to wrestle with the thoughts those men and I have wrestled with: How do these detours fit into God's plan, not only for the one God called into the pastorate, but also for those to whom he was to minister?

May each reader, whether you are one of these whose abuse still festers in my mind, bugging me at times to conduct wrongful attacks and rip away scabs over memories trying to heal from your words or actions in years past, or you're someone I've never met, may we each earnestly take a good look at ourselves. Am I one who has changed, or is changing, another's world by my own negative attitude and careless words?

Yes, some words "slip out", but Jesus made it clear that words reveal what lodges in our hearts. (Matthew 12:34, 15:18)

May God continually bless you who are intentionally an encouragement to others; you will never be able to measure the worth of your words, facial expressions or acts of kindness this side of heaven. You may have saved a ministry by your thoughtfulness.

But there are those holding these pages who would have to admit that before the words left the mouth, the heart's intention was either destruction or cutting away at the courage it takes someone else to serve the Lord with joy.

Another question to consider: Do we bring our negative scope to our worship services, focusing more on finding faults than on humbly bowing before our God of grace and mercy to worship Him?

More "self-test": Do we linger longer if we hear a criticism of the pastor, or of another brother or sister in the Lord? Do we perk up our ears when we think we are overhearing some negative whispering?

Whether you spoke or behaved toward me or another fellow follower of Christ in the manner described within this book, or wanted too, if you recognize yourself, I pray you will accept these words in the right spirit. I have found that as the Holy Spirit convicts me of my sin, the wisest course, the shortest path to peace, is to make the attitude correction and do what I can to clear the record. So quit grinding axes and start sharpening your experience with the Sword of the Word.

It takes humility to apologize. If we are sincere, and offering a humble apology to those we have offended, whether the offense was one wrong comment or years of persecution, apology not only "mends fences" between two parties, but it will also grant you more peace. I know. I have had to deal with my own guilt, too.

Facing our individual guilt is one of the first steps we take to establish fellowship with Christ. He came, after all, because our whole world was filled with sinners, and would continue to be filled with sinners like you and me as long as life on earth remains. I, and you, we are the reason Jesus suffered and died on the cross.

Though God's grace urged us to acknowledge our need to receive Jesus Christ as our personal Savior, our own faith walk as God's children begins when we acknowledge that we owe Jesus Christ an apology. He, God's sinless Son, died for us sinners, and that message was the heart of what I intended to declare throughout my ministry.

Let me tell you a little about my own early experiences within a congregation where the foundation of my spiritual life began.

I can identify with Yancey's experience described in his book, "Soul Survivor, How My Faith Survived the Church". He speaks of growing up in a church similar to my own. I grew up in a church that was very fundamental and evangelical in its teachings. We had a full week of evangelistic meetings every fall with a guest preacher who gave an invitation every night for sinners to come forward, kneel at the front pew and receive Christ as Personal Savior. It was imbedded in our beliefs that movies, dancing, make up and card paying were all sins that must be avoided. Also, you did not play ball, read the comics (save them 'til Monday) or use the scissors on Sundays. Smoking and drinking were, of course, even more serious sins. Smoking or drinking was a sign that the person is not a Christian.

Through the years I have come across many whom, as young people, left our denomination because of such teachings that I mentioned above. I, however, accepted these teachings as truth and stayed with my church.

The same church that gave me such teaching is the very same church that gave me a foundation in God's Word and led me to a saving experience with Jesus Christ. The excessively strict, narrow and dogmatic teaching I heard every time I sat in that church taught me to examine every situation and common practice against the teaching of Holy Scripture. Through the years, I have adjusted my thinking on many of the issues I was taught in the church during my youth, but I still honor my spiritual heritage and especially the pastors and the lay leaders at the time.

Though my church, like yours, consisted of regenerated sinners, I did see Christianity in action. I lost my father when I was twelve years old and will always be grateful for the man, my father's friend, who from that day on, showed special interest in me and offered encouragement each time I came to church Sunday mornings, Sunday evenings and Wednesday evenings. Without his taking time, even going out of the way, to be a friend and give encouragement I would not have experienced the spiritual growth that came to me during those formative years. His interest in me and my family continued until he too, joined that "crowd of witnesses". He exhibited the kind of character I expected to see exhibited in every congregation.

Even though others might scoff at the brand of Christianity that surrounded me in my childhood, I have concluded that without that kind of ultra-conservative teaching from my church and in my home, I could very easily have gone astray as I grew up. If I had not been well grounded in God's Word and the strict disciplines of the Christian life, it is difficult to say how I would have handled the temptations and circumstances I faced through my youth and while serving in the military. I guess I would say the teaching of my home and my church kept me on the straight and narrow path.

Later, after entering the ministry, I would experience verbal abuse and criticism, and as the title of this book implies, I wanted to see the yellow flag thrown, not only for my sake, but also for the sake of others who would answer the call to ministry. Most pastors, like I, chose to enter ministry in response to God's call, but our hearts tremble and we find verbal attacks and criticism devastating.

My call to ministry began when I was quite young, but I had another idea. I wanted to be a farmer. I loved working the soil, but most of all I loved the livestock. The animals were my friends, and they knew it. I would take naps using a sheep for a pillow. I would hug the cows around the neck and the horses on the nose. I was a very gentle, soft speaking, sort of person who loved everybody, every animal and everything. As a teen-ager, I was known around the neighborhood as the one who could handle high-strung horses. There wasn't a horse I couldn't sweet-talk and pat into settling down. It would upset me terribly if I saw a neighbor whipping or even yelling at a horse.

I did not take that call I sensed as a child seriously. After all, I was a very quiet, gentle and soft-spoken boy, as I said. I would rather be by myself than socialize with others. I was frightened beyond words as we approached Christmas because it meant I would have to get up on the platform and recite my memorized "Christmas piece". God surely must not want this shy kid in the ministry.

God's call to ministry came through very strong when I was in the military. I was in the WWII Occupation Force, still resisting that call. God surely had the wrong person here. While overseas, I finally gave a conditional acceptance of the call. I said, "Lord, OK, I'll go, but don't send me to a foreign mission field. I will be a home-land pastor if you insist". I was a stay at home kind of boy, and being on the other side of the world, which is where I was at the time made me feel even more-so. The Lord did not accept that and I had no peace.

On a Saturday night, I knelt by my bunk while poker games were going on at the other end of the shack, and prayed, "Lord, tomorrow morning, in the chapel service, do something to make it clear to me if this inner compulsion is really true".

My usual Sunday morning procedure was to go to the chapel early to read over the Scripture text and read through the hymns before the service began. That morning was no different. I read through the verses for "I Love to Tell the Story". I read in verse 3:

"I love to tell the story –
For some have never heard
The message of salvation
From God's own holy word."

My thought was, "That verse says I should be a missionary " Then I read verse 4:

"I love to tell the story –
For those who know it best
Seem hungering and thirsting
To hear it like the rest."

My thought now was, "That verse says I should prepare to become a home land pastor. But I'm safe." With this Chaplain we never sang the third verse. It was always first, second and last. Yes, always! Then the Chaplain announced this hymn saying, "We will sing the first three verses only." Can you imagine how I felt? I bowed my head right there on that military bench and prayed, "Lord. I surrender. I'll go where you want me to go." My heart was filled with peace from that point on. A few days later, in a letter from my mother, she wrote about her prayer time on Saturday night when the Lord had told her that He wants her son in the ministry. That hour of her prayer corresponded exactly to that Sunday morning hour as I sat on that chapel bench on the other side of the world and surrendered to God's call.

I sought to be obedient to God's call and leading. As the years of training proceeded, God did not seem to be leading where I thought He would. Then it came to me, my call was not necessarily to go to the mission field, but to be unconditionally yielded to my Lord and Master. I have always sought to be faithful to my Savior and Lord, but I was awakened to the realization that my first yield to God's call was conditional while He wants a totally yielded servant. I have always wanted to be sure it was God's will when we moved to a different church, and I have always wanted to be sure I would say what He wants me to say when I get into the pulpit. A lot of prayer went into sermon preparation and I always went to the pulpit with complete notes to be sure I said what God had laid on my heart through the days before.

To pray and strive to be a faithful servant of God and then have your own people point out your mistakes and weaknesses in a judgmental sort of way is devastating. Oh, yes, there is what some like to call "constructive criticism." We can call it "constructive criticism", but that is a nice term behind which to hide. Usually, it is clear through the timing and the tone of voice; that the criticism was not intended to be a positive thing for the person being criticized.

Back in elementary school we would hear some child say, "Sticks and stones may break my bones, but words will never harm me." Do not believe it. I would much rather be battered by sticks and stones than to be battered by the words and actions that have been thrown at me.

It is time that we acknowledge that verbal, physical or emotional abuses are the underlying roots of mental and emotional problems. I am convinced many of the terrible atrocities that have been committed in our society grew from times when antagonists wanted to derail the mental health of an individual over whom he felt superior.

No, I will not excuse bizarre behavior resulting from the sinful behavior of the antagonist. Each of us is accountable for the response we make. However, dear reader, sometimes I suspect we prod and poke and provoke a person toward an explosion, and then we stand back ready to judge, ignoring the taunting action leading up to the explosion.

I regret to admit, I was tempted to explode in ways that would have made the headlines, not because it was my normal personality, which it is not at all, but because of the prodding and poking I endured without defending myself.

May we all understand, at least a little better, the hearts and minds of those who commit terrible atrocities and the motivation behind such actions? None of us knows the burdens that others carry nor do we know the emotional and mental pain with which they might be living each day. Since we do not know the hearts and minds of anyone, let us be careful so we do not add in any way to their burdens.

It is not my intention to fill this epistle with all bad news. My ministry sometimes had exemplary people who prevented pastoral abuse. Those you will read about because I want readers to know how simply they can propel a ministry forward.

I again express appreciation to my wife, children and grandchildren who have endured me as I struggled with depression, depression brought on by the abuse I took from others. Thank you for your steadfast love even when I was not the person I could have been.

An example is my refusal to participate in table games. I have, at times attempted to explain why I don't want to be included, but it was obvious they did not understand. After I tried to explain, they would make remarks that to me were talking about apples while I was trying to explain oranges. They did not realize that I had experienced deep emotional wounds that caused my refusal to play table games. It was not at all as a child would say, "You hurt my feelings so I'm going home". While trying to heal, just one remark spoken, whether in jest or seriously, a remark that no one else would think of as anything but ordinary game talk, rips off the scab and the bleeding begins again. Any kind of table game, even now, awakens bad memories. Dear Family, I wish I could have participated with you more fully, but I was trapped by haunting memories that interfered with our times together.

Again, I say a special thanks to my wife, who you will see later, had to put up with my extreme responses, but who faithfully stayed with me. I wish I had been able to handle things differently, but I am grateful she and I were a ministry team and that she was someone I could trust when my world was crumbling around us.

When you, dear reader, are a part of a church, do not speak ill of the pastor, his wife, or his children and expect the pastor to preach his best. If there are issues that need addressing, take a good look at I Thessalonians 5:12, 13a, "Now we ask you, to respect those who work hard among you, who are over you in the Lord and who admonish you. Hold them in the highest regard in love because of their work." In addition, see Galatians 6:10, ". . . let us do good to all people, especially to those who are of the family of believers." as a guide to prepare your own heart before the conversation begins. You have heard it said, "If Mama ain't happy, ain't nobody happy" and you have been told not to attack the cubs of she-bear, so if you want to avoid destroying a pastor's ministry, don't attack anyone who lives in the parsonage, and I add, don't attack anyone who attends your church.

I hope you are willing to become a defender of the ministry, and I hope my words will challenge and help equip you to fulfill that responsibility. By reading my story in the pages that follow, I hope you will become one of the world's strongest defenders of pastoral ministry. Someone's eternal destination may depend upon how you, personally, and your church treat its pastor.

Points to Ponder before We Proceed

The following scriptures and questions are offered here for your reflection and discussion.

1. Let's consider these words in I Thessalonians 5:12-22.

    "Now we ask you, brothers, to respect those who work hard among you, who are over you in the Lord and who admonish you. Hold them in the highest regard in love because of their work.

    "Live in peace with each other. And we urge you, brothers, warn those who are idle, encourage the timid, help the weak, be patient with everyone. Make sure that no one pays back wrong for wrong, but always try to be kind to each other and everyone else.

    "Be joyful always; pray continually; give thanks in all circumstances, for this is God's will for you in Christ Jesus.

    "Do not put out the Spirit's fire; do not treat prophecies with contempt. Test everything. Hold on to the good. Avoid every kind of evil."

2. Do you agree that pastoral abuse, even criticism, is or can be a serious hindrance in ministry? Why, or why not?

3. How can you help prevent pastoral abuse in your congregation?

4. What encouragement do you think would be appropriate to offer to your pastor?

5. What encouragement or advice do you think would be appropriate to offer a person who has been critical of the pastor?

6. How are the pastor's spouse and children treated by "peers" in your church?

Personal challenge for the brave-hearted and obedient:

7. If, as you let God search your heart, you realize you are guilty of possibly hindering a pastor's ministry, what steps will you take to un-do the consequences?

8. Pray for your pastor several times this week and see if your attitude toward him is different when you hear him preach on Sunday.

For pastors in similar circumstances, or who might encounter similar obstacles:

The Psalms are loaded with examples of someone crying out about the unfairness of life and the enemies who are threatening to destroy plans. However, notice how God apparently lifts the spirit of the oppressed before the Psalm ends. Read until you find three such Psalms today. I guarantee you will not have to read far. Yes, the Psalms are loaded with passages to give a lift to those who have been persecuted by others. We are in good company. I say it again, the Psalms are "loaded" with such passages, but I'll just mention three that have been special to me during these times: Psalm 13, Psalm 32 and Psalm 55, especially note verses 12-14).

Chapter 2:

Biblical Basis for Being an Encourager to Your Pastor

Lest you think I am writing this to you because I have a chip on my shoulder I here emphasize the real basis for my thesis, the teaching of the Holy Spirit and how He speaks through the Holy Scriptures to tell us to seek to encourage the pastor who came to help us grow spiritually. Notice what the Bible clearly says. You may want to prayerfully ponder these passages in the coming weeks, and even, perhaps, use them for discussions when you sense your congregation is in danger of disobeying God's Word and committing pastoral abuse and as you deal with the "case studies" I present in subsequent chapters.

I have chosen the New International Version of the Bible for verses cited throughout this epistle to you, but, if you prefer, I encourage you to read these verses in your favorite version as well.

- I Thessalonians 5:12-22: "Now we ask you, to respect those who work hard among you, who are over you in the Lord and who admonish you. Hold them in the highest regard in love because of their work. Live in peace with each other. And we urge you, brothers, warn those who are idle, encourage the timid, help the weak, be patient with everyone. Make sure that no one pays back wrong for wrong, but always try to be kind to each other and everyone else. Be joyful always, pray continually; give thanks in all circumstances, for this is God's will for you in Christ Jesus. Do not put out the Spirit's fire; do not treat prophecies with contemp. Test everything. Hold on to the good. Avoid every kind of evil"

- I Timothy 5:17: "The elders who direct the affairs of the church well are worthy of double honor, especially those whose work is preaching and teaching".

- Hebrews 13:7: "Remember your leaders who spoke the word of God to you. Consider the outcome of their way of life and imitate their faith".

- "(I Chronicles 16:22 and Psalm 105:15, David's Psalm of Thanks). "Do not touch my anointed ones; do my prophets no harm"

With those verses as groundwork, permit me to do a little more teaching before I relay more about my story.

God anointed the Old Testament kings by way of the priest.

David, you recall, was God's choice to become Israel's second king. God's plan was that He, God, would be the King of Israel, but the nation kept after the prophets to convince God to allow Israel to have a king in the flesh so they could be like other nations (I Samuel, chapters 8-10)? Saul was the first anointed king. Before long, God, not the people, chose David to become Saul's replacement because of Saul's failing to be faithful and obedient to God.   Before David sat upon the throne, his trust in God's timing was tested.

Saul's shortcomings included wrongly accessing David. Saul even sought to kill the one who would become Israel's most highly esteemed earthly king. During Saul's turmoil, David had opportunities, and some would say just cause, to "touch" God's anointed king, Saul, as mentioned in Psalm 105 above, David refrained from "setting Saul straight" and usurping the throne because David recognized that God had placed, and was permitting, Saul to remain king for an appointed time.

Neither Saul nor David was perfect, but God would deal with them on His own schedule because He had set them apart to carry out His purposes for His people.

God, to this day, deals with those He sets apart, and a rebuke from God will bring about the desired change more effectively than an attack, or even advice, from a parishioner. A humble pastor wants his heart right with God and will not have peace until that is so. If you have a criticism of your pastor, talk with God about it, and not, as one did according to a pastor's information, sit in the presence of the pastor and pray that God would make the pastor realize that he should resign.

Is not the ordination the church places on a pastor quite similar to the anointing placed on an Old Testament king? It is God's doing as the ordained person is "set apart" for God's work in Christian ministry.

Anointing is not only for kings, but also for the Lord's prophets and preachers. One conference superintendent, the best superintendent I knew through my years of ministry, in speaking to the gathered conference pastors said, "Do not ever stoop so low as to become President of the United States, even if you have the opportunity. You have a much higher calling, a much more important job. You are pastors. You are servants of the Risen and Living Christ. Do not forget who you are."

Let none of us forget who our pastor is. In spite of his humanness, if he is called into Christian ministry, he will be a pastor seeking to faithfully present Jesus Christ and proclaim God's whole counsel to his parishioners.

God, personally, deals with His prophets/preachers/teachers. You can count on it. Yes, you can count on Him. Only if a pastor has gotten so out of touch with God that his life, his preaching and his teaching have become unscriptural should the church leaders perhaps step in. Consider the following examples from Holy Scripture. "Ministry" has its challenges and sometimes suffers setbacks because of those to whom one is called to minister.

Abraham (Genesis 12ff) was obedient to God even though his entire life would be completely changed (sounds like a pastor's life, doesn't it?).

Moses (Exodus 3 and 4), in spite of his serious timidity (like this writer), had to learn to trust in God's sufficiency. God sent him a Helper/Encourager, Aaron, to be at his side. Consider Moses dealing with people who were often out of sorts and liked how they had it before he was in charge. Then, again, there was Moses' suffering the consequences of losing his temper, but still being responsible for a huge "congregation". The point is that God deals with His leaders. Think about Moses' frustration when it seems his leadership/ teaching and time alone with the Lord has been wasted because his congregation has followed another's suggestion (Exodus 32).

Jesus spent much time in prayer. Pastors see the necessity of much time spent in prayer. But just as in the ministry of Jesus, the religious people today easily get wrapped up in serving the Lord and overlook taking time to consult with Him.

The Conference Superintendent came to visit with my congregation when trouble arose there over the spreading rumor that the pastor had failed to make a hospital call when he should have been there. As he was meeting with the people, one man spoke up saying, "despised and rejected by men, despised and rejected by men", the words Isaiah used to speak of the coming Messiah (Isaiah 53:3). The Superintendent told of this when he came to our house after the meeting and added, "That puts you in pretty good company".

We have the case of Jesus having to leave His own hometown (Mark 6:3) because there He was "without honor", and their "lack of faith". Pastors, we *are* in good company. This was the Jesus who willingly took upon Himself the sin that was not His own because He loved us.

Pastoral ministry is hard, but like the disciples/apostles, pastors are willing to pay the price if they can continue making progress in fulfilling God's call upon them. Just think of how much they could get done if they did not have to be paying those prices.

Points to Ponder before We Proceed

The following scriptures and questions are offered here for your reflection and discussion.

1) Re-read the scriptures located above. Why might those passages seem to carry more weight after reading this section on a Biblical Basis for Not Roughing Your Pastor?

2) This author is not claiming that a pastor is sinless. How ought the pastor apply that passage to himself and to ministerial responsibilities? (Remember, the author uses the masculine pronoun for expediency, and these questions will apply as well in the future sections.)

3) If a pastor admonishes his congregation to mature in Christ, "We proclaim him (Christ), admonishing and teaching everyone with all wisdom, so that we may present everyone perfect in Christ. To this end I labor, struggling with all His energy, which so powerfully works in me". (Colossians 1: 28-29), and others, based upon the Biblical teachings throughout the Bible, what is the likelihood of someone taking offense at the pastor's teachings? Give examples.

4) What guidelines are in place in your church so that your pastor can preach all of God's Word and do his job freely without fear of those who are watching over his shoulder and ready to criticize?

Personal challenge for the brave-hearted and obedient:

5) Are there teachings in the Bible that you want to "remove" so you can carry on your lifestyle as it is now or so you won't have to take a stand that is politically incorrect or unpopular? If so, whom are you really arguing with if you ignore the Bible's teachings?

6) When was the last time you truly repented so completely of something that offends God that your future actions were changed?

7) What would you like to have your relationship with God and His children look like? How can you take steps to make that happen?

8) I said above that religious people today easily get wrapped up in serving the Lord and overlook taking time to consult with Him. Spending at least 15 minutes a day in prayer should be expected of all who hold office in the church, Sunday school teachers and staff. Agree or disagree? Should it be a pledge included in the "Consecration of Lay Workers" service? Could we use some prodding like this now and then to remind us to do what is right?

Chapter 3:

The Making of a Pastor: My Call and Two Churches that Confirmed My Call

Where it all began:

As a child I would often have these compelling thoughts that I should be a pastor when I grew up, even to the point of having a guest preacher lay his hand on my 6 year old head and say, "This boy will grow up to be a preacher." Those thoughts and that announcement did not make a pastor of me.

In fact, the thoughts about preaching and that preacher's declaration did not make sense to me, so I would try to shove them aside. After all, I was a very shy, quiet country boy

Besides, I wanted nothing more than to grow up and be a farmer like my father of which I have written in chapter one. Though becoming a pastor was neither a desire nor a comfortable thought for me, God's call could not be ignored.

Nevertheless "a call" did not make a pastor of me, especially since I worked to ignore it. I was not like Jonah who tried to get away from God by running away. My problem was that I was just not convinced that this inner compulsion was from God. God must have the wrong person. I was not cut out for this sort of thing.

Eventually, of which I have written above, on the Island of Okinawa, while serving with the U.S. Army Occupation Troops, I surrendered fully to that call.

My Lord was very real to me in those meetings I had with Him as I walked that dark mile back to the shack from the chapel where I met almost every night with other Christian boys and also during those intimate meetings I had with Him as I sat at the little table by my bunk. Yes, I met with the Lord even when there were noisy poker games going on at the other end of the quarters, but those meetings did not make a pastor of me.

Then there was college and seminary. This education was a great help and a worthy contribution to my progress, but neither did they make a pastor of me.

But looking back, I can say I was not a "real pastor" when my wife of three years and I unpacked our suitcases and walked through the doors of the parsonage of the church I would serve. Becoming a real pastor would happen, but it had not happened yet.

So what made a pastor of me?

Church "A"

I still, to this day, look back on my first official church with deep love and fondness. The people who sat under my earliest sermons opened their doors and their hearts to me and my wife. They showed their appreciation for my attempts at declaring God's Word to them and living His principles among them, those are the people who began the process of making me into a pastor. I fondly refer to them in this epistle as "Church A". When I returned to seminary, the dean said, "I have received some very fine and complimentary reports about your ministry in Church A." To this I said, "Those people were so easy to love."

You may be someone who, right now, is making the person in your pulpit into a "real pastor". God bless you!

My denomination has a practice in which seminary students go out in the field to serve a church for a year and then return to seminary. This comes after the first year of seminary. He might go as the pastor of a small congregation or as an assistant pastor in a larger church. It is a great opportunity to get the feel of pastoral ministry before completing the training over the next two years.

I have often thanked God for my internship church. They were wonderful people.

Everyone was supportive in every way. Attendance was good. Youth ministry was effective. The children loved us. I would hear of pastors who were having troubles and I would think, "Is this church that abnormal?"

That church made a pastor of me.

The Army Engineers had been busy buying up all the land around the area surrounding and including the church, nearby farms and several small towns. The lives of the people were changing rapidly and we all knew it.

As the end of my year of internship approached, the congregation realized they would soon have to close the doors. They asked me to stay another year to see them through those difficult months ahead. The seminary dean agreed to honor their request.

During those two years there were some converts, some new people joined the church and later I would see more fruit from my labor as one of the boys from that church went into the ministry.

As I look back over my 43 years of pastoral ministry, I am aware of seven people in careers of some form of ministry, who as children and youth, sat under my ministry. My wife and I have continued lifetime friendships with some of the people from my internship church.

The one from this congregation who went into the ministry sent me a letter, not long ago, in which he wrote, "Everything that I am is because of you." Yes, there have been victories in the ministry.

Years after we had left Church A, another letter arrived from a woman who wrote in her note, "It was because of you that my boys turned out so well."

Thirty years after leaving Church A, a couple from that church drove a long distance to pay us a visit. There was much conversation, and one of the things the man said was, "During those years when you were at our church I never heard anyone speak a negative word in any way about your ministry." Thank God for churches like Church "A", but oh how things were to change.

Even more years had passed when, after retirement, a friend of mine returned from a conference annual meeting to tell me he had met a man, who noticing the name tag with home town, asked if he knew me. This man had been only a boy when I served church "A". My friend's report on their conversation sent me into tears as I recalled those good years in that church and the fact that the boy, now a middle-aged man, remembered me that well after all those years. He was from a family who had joined our church during my short two years there.

I cite those comments and notes to me, not because of any desire to boast, but because they are indicative of the unhindered ministry I was able to carry out in that congregation. Of course the Lord gets the credit for bringing his Word to life and for moving in the hearts and minds of those people, but I, a pastor called to serve them, was allowed to be his vessel during my two years there.

Do you realize that none of us can measure the blessings that came to others when congregations encourage one another and their pastor? Perhaps none of us should be so empowered by encouragement, but in our humanity, we are, and scripture urges us to be, encouragers, both by the example of Barnabas and by passages like the writings of Paul.

I say it again; it was the kindnesses, the support and encouragement of those people that made a pastor of me.

I still had two years of seminary ahead of me, and then I would accept another call to a church. Dared I hope I had become a pastor and that I understood the ministry? Dared I hope that all church/pastor relationships would be as healthy and mutually beneficial?

Church "B"

I came to Church B after graduating from seminary. Here again, I had a supportive congregation who was generous with compliments and encouragement. They did not give advice, suggest changes or offer corrections, but I learned a lot from these people just by listening to their positive conversations, and observing their actions and their work in the church. I thank God for the memories.

They also contributed much to the making of a pastor.

We had a Sunday evening service with an attendance during the summer months that was double the Sunday morning service. We were in a summer vacation area and near to a rather large and exclusive resort. The servants, cooks, governesses and chauffeurs had Sunday evenings off, so they came to church. We also saw the monetary giving to church increase enormously during those years I was there.

Having a full church is a blessing and encouragement to a pastor and faithful attendance by parishioners is "icing on the cake". A pastor's spirit can rise or fall when he steps up to the church platform, looks over the congregation and notices those who are present and those who are conspicuous by their absence.

In five of my churches, the Sunday morning attendance was greater than the membership, largely because our members were faithful and they brought their children.

Faithful attendance is always an encouragement to a pastor. You, dear church member, are important to him.

By the time we completed ministry at Church B, we were a family of five. My family and I were happy there and the ministry was going well, but I awakened every morning with a headache. My allergy doctor tried everything he could think of and finally said, "The only way you are going to get over this is to move to a different climate". I soon had a call to another church and when I tendered my resignation there was an immediate motion to not accept it. I explained the situation and they then accepted my resignation with regret.

Church "C"

Church C was a strong congregation in a small town where there were two other churches. Ours was "the church" in town, having influence upon and holding the respect of the community.

One of the other pastors in town complained, "When new teachers come to town, if they are of (his denomination) they come to my church. If they are (naming the other denomination), they go to that church. If they are anything else, they go to your church."

We did have several teachers who were more than pew warmers involved in our church.

Two of those teachers, together with two teachers not from our church, came to my office one day after school. They requested that I be a candidate for the position of Director on the school board. They said the school board desperately needed me.

I checked with the church board who said, "Go for it. They need you there."

The word got around and though a record number of voters turned out, I lost by a narrow margin in the final count and I was relieved not to be elected. The fact that someone was courageous enough to run opposite an incumbent shook up the board and some much needed changes followed. I guess you can say that although I was not elected, my running for the position accomplished its purpose.

I had a strong ministry there even though it was pretty much a routine, maintenance kind of ministry. I was beginning to sense that the Lord had another move ahead of us.

Of course, not every day as a pastor in Church C was perfect. There were times when I met some opposition.

There was a woman in that church who became very upset with me if the Sunday morning worship went over 60 minutes.

I have always been known and appreciated for my 60-minute services, but occasionally there would be something extra in the service and on those days, this woman would walk out at exactly 12 o'clock noon. I think she was more intent on watching the clock than listening to the sermon.

After this had been going on for several weeks I learned that this woman had approached the church chairman telling him he better have a talk with the pastor and tell him he must be through by 12 o'clock.

Listen to this answer by that wise chairman, "The pastor is the one who was called by God into the ministry, not I. The pastor was trained in seminary, not I. It is the pastor who has experience in the pastorate, not I. Who am I to be telling him how to do his job?"

I would say to him, "Wisely said! We need more church members like you!"

When I moved on, Church C had a farewell program to top all farewell programs. Each department head in the church gave a short talk with glowing statements about the ministry of the past four years.

The conference superintendent, who listened to the wonderful praises for the ministry we had conducted there, said, half-joking and half-serious, "It's too bad this program was not recorded so you could play it to the congregation in your next church and show them what a great pastor they got."

Here, again, was a church that contributed to the making of a pastor, but it was time to move again. I was ready for something more challenging.

So what made a pastor of me?

Yes, the college training and the seminary training was valuable, very much so, but ministry is a difficult calling. Without the support of the people in my first three congregations, I could easily have given up, especially if later experiences had come to me at this stage of my ministry.

I was still enjoying being a pastor. If being a pastor were like other occupations, then surely I was "getting the hang of it" and things would only get better, right?

I can look back now and see many good things took place that would not have happened had I left the ministry that early, but I was soon to encounter a string of much tougher days, days that made me think about quitting like many other pastors had done.

Points to Ponder before We Proceed

The following scriptures and questions are offered here for your reflection and discussion.

1. How is cooperation with co-workers and family members important in your daily life?

2. What are some times in your life when your life might have gone differently if an acquaintance had applied Philippians 4:8-9, "Finally, brothers, whatever is true, whatever is noble, whatever is right, whatever is pure, whatever is lovely, whatever is admirable – if anything is excellent or praiseworthy – think about such things.

Whatever you have learned or received or heard from me, or seen in me – put it into practice. And the God of peace will be with you", and Ephesians 4:31 and 32, "Get rid of all bitterness, rage and anger, brawling and slander, along with every form of malice. Be kind and compassionate toward one another, forgiving each other, just as in Christ God forgave you." before a chain of events began to take place?

3) What steps does your church offer to help people mature in Christlikeness?

4) How are your Christian acquaintances different from your non-Christian acquaintances in conduct and conversation, especially conversation about others? How are you different from non-Christians?

Personal challenge for the brave-hearted and obedient:

5) In what ways is the Word of God important to you as you go about your daily life?

6) In what ways are you not counting on the Sunday spoon-feeding to be sufficient for the week, but supplementing your spiritual diet so that when you get the harder-to-digest food from your pastor, your mind is ready for it?

7) Is there anyone you should speak to because that person helped you mature or have courage to take a step of obedience to God when you would have been more likely to continue rationalizing about how nonsensical the idea would have been, but which now you see was the right thing to do? You cannot know what your call, email, or note might mean to that person when times in ministry are tough.

8) If the Holy Spirit were suddenly taken away from you, what difference would it make?

9) If your Bible were suddenly taken from you, what difference would it make?

For pastors in similar circumstances, or who might encounter similar obstacles:

The Psalms are "loaded" with examples of someone crying out about the unfairness of life and the enemies who are threatening to destroy plans. However, notice how God apparently lifts the spirit of the oppressed before the Psalm ends. Read until you find three such Psalms today.

CHAPTER 4:

The Undoing of a Pastor

Church "D"

When I came to Church D, it was a young church, having had just one pastor before me. There were only 40 church members but there were 240 in the Sunday School. Members of the church went out on Sunday mornings to pick up children and bring them in. Parents were quite content to let someone take the children off their hands for a couple hours while they slept in. In some cases, the driver had to go in and help the children get dressed. The idea had been to build the church by bringing in the community's children, but the church was not growing.

I said, "Let's change our emphasis. Let's minister to families instead of just their children."

It worked.

However there is more to the story of Church D. As often happens when a new church begins they will attract some disgruntled members from other churches. Consequently, some of those coming to Church D brought in a lot of different ideas and there were members who had picked up a misunderstanding of what a church in our denomination is. There were those who tried to turn us into something that does not fit in our denomination. I stood firm for the denominational body of which I was an ordained pastor, the denomination that had planted this church and was giving financial support until it grew to be self-supporting.

There are, of course, legitimate reasons for leaving a church such as teaching false doctrine, or the pastor is not living the life he preaches. These opposing views were not unchristian, but a group within the church insisted their scriptural interpretation was superior to our denomination's teachings, especially regarding baptism and eschatology. Our differences were a matter of interpretation of Scripture.

While we practice adult baptism by sprinkling or immersion, they insisted a person was not saved until he had been immersed, making baptism a matter of obedience.

We also practice infant baptism for parents who are believers. That did not sit well at all with the opposition.

While our denomination recognizes that Scripture may be interpreted in different ways regarding the end time, a group within Church D insisted the only Scriptural interpretation was pre-millennialism.

One woman wrote a letter to our denominational headquarters reporting my positions, expecting me to be defrocked. I, of course, was standing firmly with the teaching of the denomination so her letter did not get far.

Recognizing these differences and the potential for disunity, I placed the doctrinal emphasis on Jesus Christ, wherein our unity lies, as in Colossians 1:15-23 and Galatians 3:28, which reads as follows:

"He is the image of the invisible God, the first born over all creation. For by him all things were created: things in heaven and on earth, visible and invisible, whether thrones or powers or rulers or authorities; all things were created by him and for him. He is before all things, and in him all things hold together. He is the head of the body, the church; he is the beginning and the first born from among the dead, so that in everything he might have the supremacy. For God was pleased to have all his fullness dwell in him, and through him to reconcile to himself all things, whether things on earth or things in heaven, by making peace through his blood, shed on the cross.

"Once you were alienated from God and were enemies in your minds because of your evil behavior. But now he has reconciled you by Christ's physical body through death to present you holy in his sight, without blemish and free from accusation – if you continue in your faith, established and firm, not moved from the hope held out in the gospel. This is the gospel that you heard and that has been proclaimed to every creature under heaven, and of which I, Paul, have become a servant."

"There is neither Jew nor Greek, slave nor free, male nor female, for you are all one in Christ Jesus".

Also, I pointed to Ephesians 4:10-13, which speaks of the church being built up when we all reach unity in our faith and knowledge in the Son of God, and to Colossians 1:15-23 which speaks of the supremacy of Christ over all things, persons and ideas.

To make a long story short, the 40 members soon dwindled to 20 because of those who left when they did not like where I was leading the church.

Opposing views had forced me to even more fervently search the Scriptures by which I became more firm in my beliefs. This was good for my spiritual growth, but dealing with people who could not understand why we would not become the church they believed was right, took a toll on me physically and emotionally.

At the same time, I was very tired physically and emotionally from a heavy counseling load and chairing the building committee.

That you may better understand the life of a pastor, even when his congregation is not discontent with his ministry, let me elaborate a bit to help you understand the often physical and emotional strain more clearly.

Now that we were focusing on ministering to families, the congregation was growing. We had Sunday School classes meeting in the furnace room, balcony and wherever we could find enough space in this small building that had been purchased from the congregation that had closed. Soon we decided that we needed to build. The church selected a building committee, but no one would accept the extra burden of chairing that committee. That meant either we drop the building plan or I become the chair. I took on the responsibility. I would need to stop by the construction site each day.

There was much work to be done before we could even break ground, the first major decision was, "Do we spend the extra money and hire a professional architect or do it ourselves?" That issue was divisive because some argued that we could save a lot of money by doing it ourselves, but we went the architect route. Once we broke ground, there were weekly committee meetings.

Often I was called to the building site during working hours because I was the only one available to make an immediate decision. There was the time I dropped by as the carpenters were laying the decking on that high, steep roof. I stood in what would become the sanctuary, and seeing the bottom side of the decking my thought was, "My goodness! Are we going to have to sit here for years and look up at all those cracks in the lumber?" I talked to the building superintendent, but there was nothing he could do about it. I went immediately to the architect who came out to take a look. At his order, the decking came off. The project was delayed while a new order of decking arrived.

There were many other times during this building project where I was so thankful we had chosen to use a professional architect. My voice meant nothing to the builders, but the voice of the architect carried weight because builders aren't paid until the architect approves the work.

There were sticky decisions, discussions throughout the planning stage and the building process.

Where do we place the choir? Some said the choir belongs in the traditional place in front. Others said the best place is to the side of the platform where they could be heard while not boldly in front of the congregation. Still others said the choir should be in the back of the sanctuary. "It's the music ministry that mattered, not the singers," was the argument.

Our conference superintendent settled that one for us when he said, "If you place the choir anywhere but in front of the congregation you have gone against the whole idea of television."

Next, we had to go through a similar process to decide where to put the organ and piano, which was resolved by building a partial brick wall so the organist and pianist were visible, but not obvious.

Deciding the color of the carpet was easier when someone pointed out that the color of Divinity is red. The chairman of a building committee can easily become overwhelmed by the multitude of opinions offered by church members who have various opinions as to what their place of worship should be and by "on site" decisions that must be made.

Many pastors give a week each summer to minister at Bible Camp. I was usually the speaker, the Bible teacher or the director. When there was a shortage of counselors, I would rearrange my schedule and sermon preparation to give an additional week to that ministry.

What else fills a pastor's weekday calendar? A lot of it never gets written on the calendar, it just happens because of a phone call.

I was called away from our family dinner table to go see a woman who had just been beaten by her husband. I went there immediately to find her bloody, the house in shambles and the phone cords pulled from the walls.

This was the day after I had read an article in our denominational magazine about a pastor who had been killed by the angry husband of an abused woman whom he, the pastor, was driving to a safer location. That story was on my mind as I sat in their living room, with my car parked out front and saw her husband drive by several times.

Though she had a friend in the next block, she was afraid to go out on the street. Fearing what could happen if she was seen getting into my car with me, I said, "Go there and I will be right behind you with my headlights." She made it safely to her friend's house.

Over the next few days, I had meetings with the husband. The couple reconciled and she returned home. He began coming to church. I wish I could say that he made a firm decision for Christ as his own Savior and Lord, but I did not see that happen while I was still serving there.

Another time, I was called out just after our family dinner, by a woman who said her husband was threatening suicide. She said he had not slept for three days. I sat by his bedside for a couple hours before he and I moved to the kitchen table drinking coffee, cup after cup.

At about 5 a.m. he asked, "Is it really true, all that you say about God's love and forgiveness?"

I said, "Absolutely true. God said it Himself. It is His Word that I have read to you. It is right here and you can count on it."

A few moments of silence followed, and then I heard him say, "Then I can go to bed and sleep". He got up, went to his bed and was sound asleep in just a couple minutes.

I returned to that home later that afternoon. This man looked like a new person as he met me at the door. He greeted me with "Welcome Doctor Rev."

His wife stepped up behind him and said, "Paul, he's not a doctor, he's a Reverend", to which the quick response was, "I know that, but he did more for me than all those doctors at the Mental Health Center and I'll call him Doctor."

Another woman would watch television until 2 a.m. and after going to bed would begin thinking about her miserable life. She would call me at 2:30 to begin a 2-3 hour conversation. She would not tell me who she was, but after a few weeks of this, her daughter phoned to say her mother was threatening suicide. Would I come?

We had a house full of guests celebrating my son's graduation from high school, but I left the party. I spent most of the night with her. I feel our phone visits had helped her, but after our person-to-person visit, she never called me again. When I called at her house, she would not answer the door.

I have many other stories, as do many other pastors serving other churches. It is as my doctor said, "A pastor's job is the most difficult job in the world". It is difficult physically and emotionally because of preparations for the "typical" aspects of preaching and ministerial duties and the struggles that arise out of caring for those who need help and handling the criticisms and abuse of others, I believe what he said is absolutely true. But thanks be to God, most of these difficult experiences do turn out well and therein is the joy of being a pastor.

Among those who stayed with us, there were a few who seemed to be looking for things to hold against the pastor and would talk about their discontent.

One example of my own weariness and poor health at the time occurred when I slept through an alarm clock. Though it was not my intention, to some that incident became the layman's equivalent of the pastor's unpardonable sin.

A woman had asked that I be at the hospital on a certain morning to pray with her before she went into surgery. I had prayed with her the night before, but her request was reasonable and I considered such a visit part of my typical pastoral duty. However, on that particular early morning, in my weary condition, I slept right through the alarm clock and the sounds of the children getting ready for school. Even if I had known the consequences, I think I still would have fallen asleep at the admissions desk!

She became terribly upset over my failure to be there to pray for her prior to surgery. I could understand her feelings, but surely, this was a forgivable sin.

After that oversleeping incident, a faithful woman in the church, a schoolteacher, said she had made a list of all the things a congregation expects the pastor to do. Then she added, "There is no way a school would ever expect a teacher to do so much, be prepared for that many classes and be present at that many meetings."

Ignoring the many times I *had* made it to a bedside and the host of other pastoral duties I had performed and was doing, someone decided to complain to the next in command, my conference superintendent.

God bless him, he came for a meeting with the congregation. He asked me to stay home while he met with them. Later that evening he came to our house. I opened the door and looked into the face of what reminded me of our neighbor's dog after that poor thing had been whipped. I had felt so sorry for that dog and standing there looking drained, my "superior" drew my sympathy.

He said, "Rev, I got mad." I knew the man well and could not believe that he was capable of ever getting mad.

I had not given up. I had preached Jesus Christ.

Here, however, is one example of the encouragement I received and an example of how God provides during my days at Church D.

I came to my office one morning feeling very low. My counseling load was heavy and I carried the burden of their problems to the office with me. I also felt the weight of my concern for the future of our church. I prayed, "Lord, do something to lift me out of the doldrums. I cannot minister to my people in this condition."

My office was in what had been a family dwelling across the side street from the church that we had purchased for extra Sunday School classroom space. Soon there was a knock on the door. I peered around the corner and saw, through the window on the door, a man who had all the appearance of a hobo: a thick, white, beard, a slouch hat, wearing a long, brown, well-worn coat.

My first thought was, "I am in no condition to talk to a man looking for a handout," and went back to my desk.

When he knocked again my thinking went to, "Well, maybe the man really does need help," so I opened the door.

I was surprised to hear him call me by name. I had never seen the man before. How does he know my name?

"May we talk a while?"

We sat down in the children's chapel on one of those low benches made for small children. He spoke a while in words that can be summarized thusly, "You are having a very good ministry. You are to be commended for your good work."

Then he prayed, I prayed and he was gone.

Two of my children were passing by on their way home from school for noon lunch just as the man was exiting my door. His appearance frightened my daughter who ran to me asking "Who was that?" Without thinking I blurted out, "That was an angel." Then as I gave him more thought, I concluded, "Yes, he was an angel."

Was he a real angel sent from God?

Maybe.

Angel or not, whoever he was, there has never been a doubt in my mind that he was sent by God. God does send people to lift those who are down. Maybe he will send you.

Do you know what it was about that experience that helped me most? It was not the prayer, even though that was a big help. It was not the encouragement to hang in there and keep serving the Lord. It was those words, "You're doing a great job."

We built a beautiful new church building because we chose to minister to families rather than only focusing on getting children into Sunday School. However, many pastors who are in on the building of a church will testify that a building project is physically and emotionally wearing, even if the pastor is not the "over-seer" of the construction. He, too often, happens to be within sight when questions arise.

I have to wonder how much less weary I would have been, and how much more vibrant my messages might have been and how many more visits I could have made, had I not become the "building-chairman-by-default". One might wonder if a layman in the church was ignoring God's prompting to take that responsibility, or was my covering it all part of God's plan? I do know I carried the weariness forward in my ministry.

Sometimes the bank financing a church's building project requires the church to purchase a million dollar policy on their pastor. I suspect banks have sometimes been left with bills after stress either takes the pastor's life or causes him to move away. Perhaps there is a clause covering bills in the event that a fuss stops the construction. That's worth thinking about when churches rush to expand facilities. Even if the pastor is not the building committee chair, if he, for whatever reason, drops out of the picture, the project is greatly handicapped if not halted.

After moving into our new building, I was drained physically and emotionally.

The conference superintendent stopped in to say, "We have seen that you have a special gift for bringing peace and unity back into a troubled church. That will be your ministry from now on." Little did I know then how prophetic his words would prove to be.

He then recommended me to Church E, saying this would be an opportunity to have an easier workload and rebuild for three or four years. "Then", he added, "we will have something big for you."

It has been a joy to return to Church D at times to renew friendships with the members and see how the ministry there has grown. That church is now approaching 300 members. Some of the members from our years there have told me, "You had a lot to do with this growth." I am humbled and honored for the recognition I have received for laying a good foundation for the growth there.

When I left after four years, burned out and tired, we had 60 members and a new building. We had come to a church of 40 members of which 20 left us before we started moving ahead.

However, all was not good. I was beginning to feel the emotional strain of conflict and physical weariness. The superintendent had picked my next assignment.

Did ministry get easier? Yes, and then No.

Points to Ponder before We Proceed

1. Hobo or CEO, could lifting others be your ministry? For some it's a gift, but everyone can and should do it.

2. Is our congregation mindful of all the things our pastor does? This writer usually worked a 60-65 hour week. There were times when he would go several days without an evening home with the family. The congregation had no idea of most of the ministries their pastor did.

3. A pastor's workload will naturally be heavy. What can I/we do help him carry that work load spiritually, emotionally and physically?

4. Have you considered sitting down with your pastor and talking about his spiritual, emotional and physical health and to get an idea of all that he does?

5. Pastors are not perfect. How good are you at forgiving and never bringing the matter up?

6. Read I Corinthians 12:12-30. The church is compared to a human body. It has many members, each with its own function. What happens to a human body when a member of the body fails to fulfill its God given function? What happens when each member of the Body of Christ is using his spiritual gifts and is rightly fulfilling his place in the function of the body?

7. Read Psalm 55. What was David's mood as he wrote this? Do verses 12-14, where he seems to be talking to someone else as he talks to God, tell you anything about what brought on that mood?

8. Had you been a member of church "D", would you have allowed the pastor to use his gifts as Chair of the building committee? Was this a case of one person exercising a task for which he was really not gifted in order to fill a need while neglecting his own gifts? Do you suppose someone else was neglecting his gifts by not accepting the job? Do Acts 6:1-7 say something about this?

9. Is there someone in your church whom you do not like? Would you be willing to pray for that person? Would you be willing to pray that the Lord would change your heart so you would like that person?

For pastors in similar circumstances, or who might encounter similar obstacles:

The Psalms are loaded with examples of someone crying out about the unfairness of life and the enemies who are threatening to destroy plans. However, notice how God apparently lifts the spirit of the oppressed before the Psalm ends. Read until you find three such Psalms today.

Pastor, as you consider your workload, I recommend that you take time to contemplate how you could make a "course correction". I know pastors who, after a few years of ministry, pulled out. Don't be quick to consider that option. There was a time when you were so very certain of God's call. Your weariness and depression does not cancel that call, nor do weariness and depression cancel God's presence, love and counsel. The treatment you get from others does not cancel the call even though the enemy, the devil, probably wants it to do that.

There are organizations that hold retreats for pastors in which pastors may receive counsel and encouragement. Consider locating one of those.

CHAPTER 5:

Church E, The Church Eyeing a Golden Calf

The conference superintendent did not tell me he was recommending me to another church with problems. Maybe he reasoned that since I did such a good job settling troubles in one church, I could do it again. Perhaps he didn't know it was a problem church even though his daughter and son-in-law were active members there. He said he wanted me to be his daughter's and her family's pastor.

I'm sure he did not realize what that church would do to me.

Later, when the problems came to a head, I heard from a former superintendent of that conference and two or three pastors who were familiar with that church. They all wrote something like, "That church has crucified every pastor they have had. I really did not think it would happen to you. I'm so sorry."

Negative news, especially news of a pastor in trouble, travels fast.

During my time at that church, the church chairman would get letters from a former pastor who was bemoaning the treatment he received there and sought an apology from the congregation. I don't think the chairmen or any other member of the congregation ever gave that apology.

I told myself I would never write a letter like that, and I have not. When I left a problem church, I left it. The problem was that it did not leave me. The troubles in those churches never left me. The memories lingered.

My wife often comments that she is so amazed at how I can remember so much from the past, even many years back. That might be a good trait, but I have many memories I would like so very much to be rid of.

I had three very good years in Church E before trouble broke loose, my ministry went well. The congregation was happy. I was happy, my wife was happy, and our five children were happy.

Then it happened.

A son of the church, after several years with a para-church organization, came home to join his father and brothers in their business. He held meetings in homes, with people from my church, of which I was unaware at the time. He promoted ideas like, "The sooner we get rid of all pastors and close up the churches, the sooner Christians can begin doing what they are supposed to be doing."

I hasten to explain that he did not get those ideas from the organization with which he had been working.

When I heard about the ideas he was promoting, the interest it was stirring up within my congregation and that I had intentionally been kept uninformed of these meetings, the emotional defeat I had when I left Church D began to flare up.

This man had several relatives in the church, and having a lot of charisma he was able to sell his ideas to a lot of people.

In a state of deep depression, I went to bed one night fully expecting not to be alive to see the sunrise in the morning. After settling into bed, I told my wife to be sure to tell the children that I love them dearly.

There were four wonderful men, one of them being the former superintendent's son-in-law, who stayed by my side during this entire difficult time. They made sure one of them would be near a phone at all times so I could reach immediate support when needed. Two or three times a day one of them would stop by to see how I was doing. Through the years I have continued to thank God for those men.

It was at this point that I developed a fear of telephones. So often when the phone rang, whether at home or at the office, I would be faced with a stressful situation. The result of some people using the phone as a means of telling me a few things, some even doing so without revealing their identity, I developed a serious case of telephobia. That fear lingers to this day. For many years to follow, if anyone dialed our house and heard me answer the phone, it meant I was the only one home. If my wife answered the phone and the other party asked for me, I would go to the phone with fear and trembling. When she began to ask, "Whom shall I say is calling?" that helped. I'm sure my blood pressure rose a few points each time I heard the phone ring. After 40 years, I have begun to have some victory over that fear, but I still avoid using the phone whenever possible. I would rather drive across town to talk to someone than call that person on the phone. Now, in these days, I am thankful for "Caller ID" and email.

After a year of continuous conflict, the church terminated my ministry there.

Having nowhere to go, and no income, I made a request that my family be allowed to remain in the parsonage until we have a place to go, or until the next pastor needs the house.

My request was denied. The superintendent hit them on that one.

What they told me later was that they had misunderstood my request. The request I made was simple and very clear. How could it be misunderstood?

When we finally did move away, some members also left the church. In later correspondence from a couple of those families we understood that they left in order to make a statement in our support.

Because people left when we left, I became known as the pastor who split the church.

Ironically, after we had been terminated, the man whose behavior started dismantling my ministry and congregation at Church E by suggesting Christians ought not to have pastors, later apologized to the church, admitting his ideas were wrong. Then he moved out of the community leaving behind a severely damaged church.

In one conversation I had with this man I referred to a book, "The History of Preaching" by Dargan, that was required reading in seminary. I pointed out that the Church of Jesus Christ was strongest at such times when preaching was strong. This surprised him.

It would have been so good, so helpful, for me to have heard his apology, but it never came my way. Had he realized the depth of the wounds I bore, perhaps he would have had enough heart to have done so. He realized he had damaged the church, but apparently he did not realize how he had wounded me. Perhaps he could move away and forget what had happened, but a pastor cannot move away and forget what took place in his church. When a congregation terminates a pastor's ministry, the congregation can put the whole incident aside and move on. The pastor whose ministry was terminated cannot do that. The congregation might think the matter is finished, but for that pastor there will always be that bleeding wound or at least a painful scar. Some years later, I spotted Church E's present pastor at a conference. Noticing his nametag, I put out my hand to introduce myself. As soon as I introduced myself as a former pastor of his church, he gave me an odd stare, dropped my hand, turned his back and walked away.

I wondered what he had been told. Surely a brother pastor could have said something like, "Let's sit down and have a talk," or, "Tell me about your experiences at Church E."

No, he simply walked away.

Did the ministry get easier? Yes, and then, No.

Points to Ponder before We Proceed

1. When Moses was in the midst of his "ministry", he spent time on the mountaintop getting instruction from God so the Israelites could more perfectly follow him. While Moses was meeting with God, his helper, Aaron, let the people persuade him to build a golden calf to have something to worship, largely because the people got tired of waiting for Moses and they were not sure he was going to return at all from his time with God (Read Exodus 32). How would you compare the human response of Moses to the human response of "Rev" when Rev's congregation began going in another direction, following another leader?

2. Which are you more likely to be, or experience, in the church you attend, those who, like the four men, are ready to inconvenience themselves to make certain the pastor knows he has loyal friends, or someone who might be tempted to pull people toward, or join with those heading toward, another form of ministry? What does interest in another form of ministry indicate about those who are ready to leave? What would you advise your pastor to do if a similar circumstance happened in your church?

3. The person who began the "split" in the church later apologized to the church body, which was probably difficult. How can the body of Christ improve on making the "road to restoration" easier?

4. If you had been the pastor, what would have kept you in ministry?

For the brave-hearted and obedient:

5. We are to fellowship with each other in gentleness and truth. What scriptures might you use if you become aware of a schism developing within your church body? What steps would you take based upon the scriptures?

6. There are, of course, pastors who do not deserve to lead a church. What are the qualifications you believe the Bible makes essential for someone who is to stand in the pulpit? Are you aware of any pastorate dismissals over the Biblical essentials?

7. What Psalm or other scriptures would you have wanted to read to the pastor if you had been one of his loyal friends, and how might you have helped bear the burden he and his family were carrying during this time?

For pastors in similar circumstances, or who might encounter similar obstacles:

The Psalms are "loaded" with examples of someone crying out about the unfairness of life and the enemies who are threatening to destroy plans. However, notice how God apparently lifts the spirit of the oppressed before the Psalm ends. Read until you find three such Psalms today.

Chapter 6:

The Sustaining Calm and the Church with Bulldozers in the Pews

Church F, the Sustaining Calm

It is very nearly impossible for a pastor to get a call to another church if he is known, even though falsely, for having had trouble in a former church. The rumors of conflict in a church travel far and wide, and the pastors almost always get the blame. After all, you have to blame someone, don't you? "Wrong!"

Why does any one person need to get the blame? Because the pastor is the leader, people conclude that he is the problem.

The conference superintendent met with a church where he thought I would fit in well. He laid it on the line with that church and said, "Yes, 'Rev' had trouble where he is now, but he is innocent of any kind of wrong doing. Some people in the church made his life very difficult. He can be a good pastor for you."

They gave me the call.

This church became a welcomed interlude between two very difficult charges. During my years there, I had several weddings and there were those of my church who married spouses from other churches. In every case, with just one exception, the newlyweds settled into our church. One of our daughters married the son of the church chairman while we were there, and we count others from that church as lifelong friends.

However, I arrived at Church F under a deep depression that hung on for five years. There were days when I would "hibernate" in the upstairs back bedroom while my wife was at work and the children were in school. If people came to the door, I would ignore them. I was in no condition to talk with anyone.

I tried to read, meditate and pray. Even meditation and prayer are difficult when one is depressed. Even Bible reading is difficult,

I took some comfort in reading about the Canaanite woman in Matthew 15:21-28. The scriptures tell us her life's circumstances had her at the depths of despair. She even felt pushed aside when she talked to Jesus. She was so low that all she could do was to say to Jesus, "Lord, help me!"

Even that simple prayer left her with a response that sank her deeper into despair. She did not give up, and Jesus helped her.

How did I get victory over depression? Please take note, now, of what I say. The Lord answered my simple and faltering prayer and laid it on the hearts of a few people in the church to say good things to me.

They would often compliment what I did. They loved my sermons. They were so very appreciative of my work and said so.

I also received help from some of Robert Schuller's writings.

After five years of ministry in Church F, I began to make fairly good recovery.

Church F was a solid church, well grounded in the denomination and had been effective in the community for 90 years. Nevertheless memories of my previous experiences continued to haunt me. After eight years, the Lord laid it on my heart that I was ready to move on to something bigger and more challenging. So it was to move again.

As for the something bigger and more challenging, Wow! Did I get just that!

Church G, The Church with Bulldozers in the Pews

Hoping for another long-term and even more successful pastorate in our new call, we purchased a home so we could become more established in the community. By now, we were a family with two children in junior high and high school. Of the others, one was working, another in college and the third was married.

We weren't exactly met by the community's "Welcome Wagon".

A man came to me right after the morning service on my very first Sunday and said, "You don't belong here."

Wow! That hardly sounds like a "welcome" greeting. He went on to tell me that half the congregation still considers my predecessor as their pastor, but the other half of the congregation was responsible for driving him away.

My thought immediately went to, "Not again!", while under my breath I prayed, "O Lord, why me?" I remembered those words of my former superintendent, "We have seen that you have a special gift for bringing peace and unity back into a troubled church. That will be your ministry from now on."

I often wondered why this man, a professional with a Master's Degree, felt he needed to give me that report on my first Sunday and why I needed to be told at all. A man of his intellect, and with his experience in dealing with people of all kinds, surely would know better than to give such a curt greeting on his first meeting of a new pastor. This man who spoke those, "You don't belong here" words was a thorn in my mind, my heart and my soul through all of the six years I was there.

But, what harm can one church member do?

Oh, let me count the ways!

No, actually I will cite just a few that validate the concern we ought to have about stopping abuse before it starts. Again, I am not saying that pastors are sinless, but I do believe if a pastor is prayed for by his congregation and if he is able to soak his mind with God's Word so he can listen to God's instruction, the Holy Spirit will overcome legitimate concerns others may raise about the imperfections of a very human pastor.

Dear Christian, pray for your pastor as though your spiritual maturity depended upon it, which it does! Pray for him as though his spiritual maturity depended upon it, too, which it does. Those who oppose the work of the pastor are praying against him, and some align themselves with the greatest forces of evil to defeat Christianity while thinking they are supporting the Christian faith.

What could please the enemy more than to render pastors "useless" and "ineffective"? Is not the goal of Satan to either keep people from turning their lives over the Lordship of Jesus Christ or to stymie the witness and effectiveness of those who are Christ's servants? He will even use unsuspecting Christians to accomplish his purpose.

Ministry, even becoming a Christian, is serious business and until we leave for Heaven, we are called to live our lives in the enemy's territory. The Christian life is not for namby-pambies! I dare say that if you are not feeling a little heat from the enemy's fire, there's a good possibility you are walking too far from the center of a vibrant fellowship with Jesus Christ. The devil will not worry about you.

After I had been in church "G" a while, he, the "Thorn", which is how I had come to think of this man, came to a diaconate meeting with a list of more than 200 names which he claimed I had driven away from the church. I did not recognize any of the names on that list except for a couple I thought I might have met at one time or another. He apparently had failed to notice that our Sunday attendance at that point had doubled during my ministry there.

This man's negative attitude toward me was contagious. It spread to those who get their pleasure out of finding things for which they can criticize the pastor. Or maybe they feel it their duty. When they hear negatives, they love to "build" on those and spread the word.

One woman announced to all present at a church business meeting, "'Rev's' sermons are empty and meaningless. I don't get a thing out of them."

Two people who, just that week had mailed me notes thanking me for my sermons saying, "Your sermons have been so timely and helpful," were present to hear this verbal attack.

I sat there waiting for them to speak up, but they remained silent.

Why do those who criticize the pastor do so publicly, while those who compliment and show the pastor appreciation do so through notes in the mail?

The woman who criticized my sermons at that church business meeting phoned my wife the next morning and said, "I'm sure my words hurt the pastor, but God told me to say it".

I received many favorable notes, but those who were positive and supportive were unable to counteract the criticism spreading through the church with the help of "Mr. Thorn". The supportive folks kept quiet when criticisms were spoken. It is as Anne Dillard writes, as quoted by Philip Yancey in "Soul Survivor" (p. 239), "If

Christianity is true, why on earth don't we act like it? Does anyone have the foggiest idea what sort of power we so blithely invoke?"

With all of this conflict, this bulldozing, going on, I sank back into depression. My long-nurtured and sometimes too well fed feelings of low self-esteem returned. I would think, "I should never have come here!" However I must say that there were a few bright spots. There were two families who stood solidly with me and let it be known, but their voices were like leaves in the wind. A couple other families were very quiet. I never did know where they stood on this issue.

Then I would be reminded I had come to Church G because God called me there. That was small comfort. It meant I was letting God down.

Those thoughts sank me even deeper into despair. I would spend hours in my office. I could not force myself to get out and take care of visitation in the way I had done at first, no matter how I kept telling myself to get going and no matter how much I prayed about it. I spent hours just walking up and down the aisles of the church and around the fellowship hall, punishing myself for my negligence, and yet I just kept walking.

I needed someone to come and remind me that Moses led his people in the face of opposition, or that Elijah, with whom I could identify, also felt his lonesome call was too hard to bear. Elijah sat under a broom tree praying that he could die. I lied on my bed one night fully expecting to die. I needed someone to extend a hand down into the pit where I was falling without my armor properly attired. I needed someone to help lift me up, or at least tell me he was looking for a ladder.

If you have experienced depression's grasp, you perhaps realize the captive can rarely devise his own escape and relying upon God for rescue seems too far away.

The enemy is skilled at entrapping us. Since I heard no one coming along side (the two families supporting me had not yet revealed their stand), and no one caring that I was descending into the pit, my mind continuously rehearsed my failures, enlarged my perception of my very human shortcomings, and deflated the memories of the blessings God had granted through my faithfulness.

The enemy was winning and I gave little thought to his being a part of the picture. He had distracted me so that I was focused upon the people who were "the problem", keeping me from realizing I was not wrestling against flesh and blood. (Ephesians 6)

People began to notice my negligence.

I longed so desperately for someone in the church to come to me and say something like, "We notice that you have been pretty down lately and that your ministry is slipping. Could we sit down and talk about it?" That did not happen, I got only criticism, and I, in my emotional state, could not bring myself to ask for such a meeting, especially if Mr. Thorn would be present.

Oh, there were meetings all right. Some would choose to talk to my wife and tell her what a poor pastor her husband was. One woman took her out for lunch. I thought this might be a sign of better things, but no. How can anyone enjoy lunch while listening to all that criticism of her husband coming from across the table, all without basis?

There was that committee meeting where a couple members of the group verbally attacked me. As we ended a long and difficult evening, it was agreed that this discussion not be spoken of to anyone at all outside of this group, not even spouses, and that we meet the following week. Next day it seemed everyone in the congregation knew about how the pastor had been attacked the evening before. The group members knew immediately what had happened. One committee member's wife was well known for her gossip and "tell all" reputation.

At the next meeting the "leak" was addressed. That man became angry saying, "I'm not going to sit here and take this!" and headed for the door.

As he was leaving I said, "I sat here and took it from you people last week. Surely you can do the same now."

He stopped in his tracks, paused a moment and returning to the table said, "I guess I can't argue with that."

Despite my depressed condition, the preaching continued quite well. My wife said she could not understand how I could stand before this congregation Sunday after Sunday and give such good sermons. Anything good had to be the Lord's doing.

The rest of my ministry continued to bump along the rocky road, though many days were without open abuse. My sympathizing family was able to establish solid friendships with members in spite of the occasional open attacks against me. Some of their friendships continue to this day. I rejoice in the fact that the Lord was bringing about positive outcomes in the midst of the mental and emotional turmoil I was facing. I also rejoice because today all of our children, now married and have their own families, are active and committed Christians in their adult lives and are married to active and committed Christians. My wife and I praise the Lord that the enemy did not triumphantly get his hold on them to draw them from their commitment to the Lord. Our family now numbers 26, all of them born again and committed Christians, including six who are in careers of Christian ministry.

There was that Sunday evening service in church "G" where I was giving a series on understanding spiritual gifts. I was well prepared and keyed up for that message. Then I noticed that a leading member of the church, who was always present and on whom I depended heavily, was not present. I don't remember why, but I really wanted him to hear this sermon. By the time I was to begin the sermon, I fell apart. I collapsed mentally and emotionally. I left the platform and slipped down the back stairs where I sat in a dark classroom. As I recall, only my wife came looking for me.

It had been my intention for some time to give my resignation, but I was postponing it in the hope of having a call to another church

(Dream on, brother!) and then to get the house sold. I also hesitated to submit my resignation because we wanted to stay until after our youngest child, a high school senior, had graduated. Who wants to move their child in the middle of the senior year?

The conference superintendent was of no help whatever. He said what the superintendent at Church E" had said, "We'll move you, and then we'll move in and take care of the problem." That is the easy way out for superintendents: Move the pastor out; then the problem settles down. However that apparent peace will last only for a while.

Why can't superintendents, who are church counselors, but also the pastor to pastors, come to the church, hear both sides of the issue and discuss the solution to the problem while the pastor is still there? The problem, the elephant in the church, needs to be addressed or else when the next pastor comes, it's only a matter of time until the problem flares up again. That is how it had worked, I came to realize, in church "E". It's a vicious circle, like the old adage about not fixing the leak in the roof when it is not raining because then there is no need to fix it. Would I be justified in warning that destructive rainstorms are just over the horizon for churches that do not address the problems?

Churches seem more guilty of neglecting to address a problem than most other organizations, perhaps because of fearing the "voluntary membership" consequence if some are offended. The truth is that voluntary members are at least as likely to pull away if the problem is not addressed. The other option is that the church will call and crucify many pastors, each of whom will likely leave in a wounded state.

Or perhaps superintendents also believe most problems are the pastor's fault.

After six years in this church, everything fell apart. I was told to resign.

I had waited too long. I received an envelope from my superintendent in which he had written my letter of resignation and included a schedule. He told me to sign it and give it to the church.

Wow! That letter certainly did not give me the feeling of encouragement or the support I would have expected from the one pulling for me to have a successful ministry in one of his congregations.

When a church has a reputation, like Church E, for having crucified every pastor who has served there over the past several years, how can a superintendent assume that moving the pastor out will settle the problem?

Well, perhaps, if I were the superintendent, I would do the same thing. Who really has enough guts to walk among moving bulldozers driven by people in blindfolds?

The words of Psalm 55:12-14 now became especially meaningful: "If an enemy were insulting me, I could endure it; if a foe were raising himself against me, I could hide from him. But it is you, a man like myself, my companion, my close friend, with whom I once enjoyed sweet fellowship as we walked with the throng at the house of God."

I read that passage at my last congregational business meeting with that church, but the days prior to that last meeting were not pleasant.

We owned a house, but how could we make payments without an income? So, again, we had no place to live and no place to go.

Soon I had a couple opportunities to candidate in other churches. In each case, I felt the interviews with the search committee went very well, but no church gave me a call. Was it because my emotional condition kept me from presenting myself as a good candidate, or had they heard that I had been in "trouble in every church I served"?

I had to conclude that the word had gotten around, especially, it seemed, in the superintendents' council. It seems there's something that makes people like to believe negative stuff. If the negative stuff is about a pastor, it becomes especially juicy, and, sadly, it is sometimes true that one's fellow pastors are among the quickest to become betrayers. That happened to me at this time. My dear colleagues in ministry, "It ought not to be so among us."

I regrettably and gradually learned that when the troubles came to a head in Church G, some members of my church phoned other pastors within our denomination to complain about me. In each case of which I became knowledgeable, the pastor sided and sympathized with the caller. I thought these men were my brothers. Could they not at least have contacted me and asked what was happening in my church? They surely knew not to put confidence in every negative thing said about another pastor. And, surely, these pastors were knowledgeable of these kinds of problems. Or, did they also enjoy the juicy gossip because hearing about pastors in trouble makes another pastor feel better knowing he is not alone, or, perhaps, pastors hearing about brother pastors in trouble makes them feel superior since they, themselves, are not experiencing problems at this time. Is that the way it works?

What about internalizing James 1:26?

We pastors also need to guard our ears and mouths and hearts, for we, more than those who sit in the pews to hear us proclaim God's Word, know we are sinners saved by grace.

Now, again, what church will call a pastor who has a reputation for having had trouble "everywhere he has been", even though such an exaggeration ignores the "successful" ministries in other churches? Do those calling pastors not realize that even the Apostle Paul was in trouble in some of the places where he worked? I would like to tell every church member, even all the world, to make no judgments until you have all the facts. But then, you have heard that before, haven't you? Do we practice it?

I was in deep depression in which I lived each day for nearly a year. I blamed myself for the troubles. I tried my best to break loose from my shackles, but I was not Samson. Because I could not break free, the criticisms built up.

Now, dear reader, please do not say that if I had had enough faith, God would have broken the shackles of depression. I had faith in God, but my spirit, emotions and mind had been severely damaged by the people I loved and come to serve. Who can question David's faith or Elijah's faith, and yet they had some serious "down times" in their ministries.

I was blaming myself for the troubles. I was willing to accept any blame for anything for which I was responsible. By now I really could not blame the church for wanting to be rid of me.

Why do they want to be rid of me? My reasoning went like this as I sometimes joined in the chorus calling for my own crucifixion:

How did I become the person I am, negligent of duties and so very depressed?

How did I become a failure in the call God gave me?

Then my thought would go back to Church E, which, together with the experiences of the past several months, caused me to recognize the truth. I alone did not deserve all the blame. The truth soon drowned in another round of self-condemnation for falling into the pit of depression that bound me so I could not efficiently carry out my pastoral duties.

This depression has stayed with me, hanging still over my head as I write these many years later. One day, in my retirement, as I was lower than usual in my depression, I said to my wife, "I really should have been able to handle those problems back in Church G." There I was, still placing the blame back on myself.

Yes, I failed, but why did I fail? Forgive me for sharing the blame, but I ask you, why was I, why am I, still so depressed? Through the years, my thoughts have often returned to those experiences in Church G, but not without shifting between self-blame and blaming others. Then I have to remind myself that I would not have gotten into such a deep depressed state had it not been for the treatment members of my church gave me.

If you, fellow pastor, suspect you are struggling with depression, make bold moves to get help, and medication if necessary, before you slide further down into the enemy's pit. The enemy will cleverly seek to keep you away from help because he knows you will be more effective when you're out of the pit, but you didn't enter ministry to be bound by that despicable creature. Today you're out of the pit, but you didn't enter ministry to be bound by that despicable creature. Today, more resources are available than when I stared up from the pit and saw no one. If your physician, your denomination or friends cannot advise you on how to climb out and away from the pit, search on the internet for pastoral counseling services. You are not the only one going through a tough call. You deserve to be freed to a fuller ministry, and remember, it was God who called you because He saw who you could be for Him!

I have attempted to talk about my depression with a few, and I suppose I come across as one who always blames others for his troubles. I am not one of those, nor do I want to be. I am willing to accept the blame for which I am responsible, and I could make quite a list of my shortcomings, but I have concluded I would have been a much better pastor and a much different person had I not had to take so much harassment from other Christians.

But, back to my pastoral journey.

Words of the turmoil at Church G began to spread throughout the denomination, but especially within the conference.

I began getting phone calls from other pastors going through similar troubles. They did not call to encourage me. They were in no condition to give encouragement. They hoped, because we were suffering through similar situations, that I would be able to give them encouragement and advice. It is because of their abuse, and the abuse of others like them, that I am telling my story.

About fifteen years after leaving church G, my wife received a letter from the church inviting her to a week of celebration of the congregation's anniversary. This hurt us deeply. They were making a sharp and obvious, "We don't like you" statement, and though it was indirect, inconsiderate and tactless, their point was clear to me. Why did they feel they even needed to invite my wife? It was clear that they wanted to make a statement to me. I sent them a greeting saying, essentially, "I see in a letter you sent my wife that you are having a week of celebration. She and I wish you well."

By the way, I understand no one ever had the courage and spiritual insight to alter the pastoral abuse that continued at Churches E and G. It saddens me to realize the enemy's foothold kept other pastors from fuller and more fruitful ministries in those congregations.

The greatest change to me personally, as a result of serving church G was that I developed a terrible fear of criticism, a fear that has hung on to me ever since.

Take note of that "immobilization" as you read the rest of my story. When I say "fear", I am talking about a deep, strong emotion that controls me. I go to pieces, emotionally, when someone criticizes me. Even simple little statements like, "Why do you have it so hot in here?", "Do you really need the TV that loud?" "Why don't you park closer to the curb?" will upset me for days. When I hear others criticized, I have strong feelings of, "My heart reaches out to you."

Criticism is a not so subtle form of rejection. By human nature, we all hate rejection, but with my experiences, any form of rejection is deeply devastating. The rejection I experienced at Church G greatly affected my ministry from then on and remains as a thorn for me to deal with even to this day.

Church "G" has not done well since we left them. I am sure their fingers are pointing at me, but I will not accept the blame. Discounting whatever had been going on in that church prior to my arrival, the trouble began on my very first Sunday when I was told, "You don't belong here".

Points to Ponder before We Proceed

1. Do you have a good answer to this question which I raised in the chapter above? Why do those who criticize the pastor do so publicly, while those who compliment and show the pastor appreciation do so through notes in the mail?

2. Rejection is a serious affront to another's personhood. The natural, survivor response is to become defensive. So I ask you, why do we criticize, which is a form of rejection? I think of a man who seems to enjoy criticizing. He criticizes the way people park their cars out front of the church. He criticizes people (to others, but not to them) who sit at the end of the pew and not go to the middle. He criticizes in many other ways. Why?

3. Jesus tells us in Matthew 7:1, 2, "Do not judge, or you too will be judged. For in the same way you judge others, you will be judged, and with the measure you use, it will be measured to you." You might say you only offer constructive criticism in order to be helpful. Discuss how constructive criticism differs, if you can, from judging another in a way that makes the critic look better than the one receiving the criticism.

When we say we are giving constructive criticism are we using those words as a "cop out"? We must examine our motives. Perhaps our real motive is that we like to criticize. Are we really trying to help a person or trying to make ourselves look better? Are we really trying to enhance and strengthen another's ministry or tear it down? You are doing one or the other. Do we seek to be the Holy Spirit's helper in growing a person deeper in Christ or do we just want to justify ourselves? It is so easy to hide behind the excuse of "I was only trying to help" or "God told me to say it". Did he, really?

4. How do you decide between whether you are the one responsible for delivering the constructive criticism or if God wants you to leave the correction to the Holy Spirit?

5. In chapter 1 the writer refers to those who seem to think they have a Divine call to keep the pastor humble. He also says there seems to be at least one in every church. You have probably known one or two. Why do some people get to be like that?

6. A question asked in the chapter above is, "Why do those who criticize the pastor often do so publicly while those who have good things to say do so through a note in the mail?" Why is this so?

7. Reread Elijah's desperation in I Kings 19 and draw parallels between his fear and frustration and the depression you read as a pastor tells his story in this chapter. How might you pray for and encourage someone you know who serves in ministry

8. Comment on this statement in chapter 4. "If you have experienced depression's grasp, you perhaps realize the captive can rarely devise his own escape and relying upon God for rescue seems too far away. What can you do for another in such a situation or condition?

9. Which is better? Driving a pastor away and perhaps ruining his ministry or hurting a few members of the church and causing their departure? This writer is thinking of a church where a group of members became

very critical of the pastor and openly called for his resignation, but several in the church stood by him. The critics finally gave up and left. It made quite a hole in the attendance and membership, but the congregation then experienced a spiritual renewal as that pastor led them through a time of healing.

10. What makes people prone to pick up on negative rumors?

For the brave-hearted and obedient:

11. How would you answer these questions the pastor of this book asks: "Do we seek to be the Holy Spirit's helper in growing a person deeper in Christ or do we just want to justify ourselves? It is so easy to hide behind the excuse of, "I was only trying to help," or "God told me to say it." We must examine our motives. Are we really trying to build a person up? Are we really trying to enhance and strengthen another's ministry or tear it down? You are doing one or the other.

12. What resources can you find for pastors who are "battle weary", and how can you share and/or support those ministries?

13. How has this pastor's story "humanized" the persons who stand in the pulpits of your community? Does that cause you to empathize with the pastors or become more judgmental of the possibility that they will be deeply affected by criticism, and what are you going to do about it?

14. A denominational administrator once told those gathered at conference, "If you don't like your pastor, it says more about you than it does about him." Could this be said about not liking the sermons, the music, or any number of things a church member might not like?

15. Would you pray daily for your pastor, not praying for him to be what you think he should be, but praying for his walk with the Lord, his sensitivity to the Holy Spirit and to the needs of the sheep of his fold?

14. There were those who stayed out of the church fray by their silence, trying to be neutral. Maybe in their hearts they stood with the pastor, but because of their silence the pastor saw them as standing with the opposition. Can one possibly remain neutral when there is trouble? Can one possibly remain neutral when there is someone who desperately needs support and encouragement?

For pastors in similar circumstances, or who might encounter similar obstacles:

The Psalms are "loaded" with examples of someone crying out about the unfairness of life and the enemies who are threatening to destroy plans. However, notice how God apparently lifts the spirit of the oppressed before the Psalm ends. Read until you find three such Psalms today.

"World Challenge" of Lindale, Texas publishes a regular mailing called "Pulpit Series" written by Gary Wilkerson which is helpful to pastors in any situation. You can get it free of charge or you can make a voluntary contribution.

Bible Camps and Christian Retreat Centers are usually willing to let a pastor have a cabin for a week or so to use for study, meditation and spiritual rebuilding. They might even give you free meals in the dining hall.

There are Church Retreat Centers such as those of The Roman Catholic Church. I have found them to be very congenial in giving Christian pastors of any denomination a room and the use of the chapel and grounds for a period of time.

For even more consideration:

Why are we so reluctant to throw the yellow flag on church members who have been guilty of "Roughing the Pastor"? Can you accept the answer that there are times when amputation of a member of the body is the answer?

The church has Scriptural authority over her members, see Hebrews 13:17. In Acts 16:4 and throughout the book of Acts we see that the mother church in Jerusalem had authority over the young churches. Matthew 16:19, 18:18 and other passages suggest to us that Jesus gave his disciples a lot of authority. So how is the church to use this authority when there are those who make trouble in the church and hinder her progress?

First of all, the church is to exercise love and kindness to all, see II Timothy 2:25, 26, but, as in disciplining a child that love and kindness has to be expressed in firm and not so pleasant ways. But the church is also to be firm. "Tough Love" it is called. In II Corinthians 13:2 the Apostle Paul is exercising authority when he writes, "I already gave you a warning . . . I now repeat it . . . On my return I will not spare those who sinned earlier or any of the others". The Apostle writes further in verse 10, "This is why I write these things when I am absent, that when I come I may not have to be harsh in my use of authority – the authority the Lord gave me for building you up, not for tearing you down".

In chapter 5 of I Corinthians, Holy Scripture makes in very clear that when a member of the church persists in immorality he is to be excommunicated from the church. "Immorality" includes a multitude of sins. On hearing the word, "immorality" we think of sexual sins, but there are other sins of equal and even greater seriousness that are immoral. Anything in words, actions, attitudes, etc. that cause division in the church, or even weaken the effectiveness of another Christian thus hindering the ministry and progress of the church are immoral. "Expel the wicked man from among you". I

Corinthians 12:13. Read Romans 12:12-31 and II Corinthians 13. Is there a difference between ruining someone else's life through sexual immorality and ruining some one else's life through criticism and rejection?

Paul writes to Pastor Titus in Titus 3:10, "Warn a divisive person once, and then warn him a second time. After that, have nothing to do with him. Anything divisive, anything hindering the progress of the church, is to be treated by excommunication from the church. Paul, himself, practiced that. See I Timothy 1:18-20. Are there not times when the church must practice spiritual amputation of body parts?

Does this harmonize with the teaching of Jesus? It most certainly does. Read Matthew 18:15-17. Upon reading that passage one will immediately sit up, take notice and say, "Why, that is exactly backwards from the way we do it." But who is backwards, we or Jesus?

CHAPTER 7:

It Takes More than Good Wishes to Rescue Pastors from the Pit

Church "H"

We had no income, no money in the bank.

We had sold our car, but most of that money would go into the U Haul truck we would have to rent with our own resources.

We had no place to go.

With our two youngest children away in college, my wife and I moved back to our hometown. Perhaps getting back to relatives and long-time friends would help.

The move from Church G to our hometown was quite a long distance, making the bill very high for two unemployed people.

Was it fair that we had to cover the expenses of moving away from the congregation who threw us out with the "blessing" of the superintendent?

Fair or not, we would pay the bill. Generally, the church to which the pastor is moving pays the bill, but since we could not seem to get on anyone's radar screen, we decided our wisest choice was to move back to our hometown.

Later, that conference did send us a check. We learned, however, that the check came, not because of compassion or that they were trying to help us, but because they were looking out for themselves. They explained that if they did not help, other pastors considering a call to their conference would be less likely to come if they heard conference leaders looked away and covered their ears when congregations told pastors to pack and move at their own expense.

Of course, God would not let us starve. He always keeps track of our address, even when we are not sure what it should be. Though we are sometimes beaten down, we still carry within us the message that others need to hear.

Before long, back in our hometown, a door of ministerial opportunity began to open to me when a church of another denomination realized there was an unemployed pastor in town. I was invited to serve as their interim pastor while they continued their search for their next pastor.

I was encouraged just by being asked. I was now preaching at Church H.

Church H's congregation further encouraged me as they expressed their appreciation for me. They were spiritually hungry and liked the food I could offer them through God's Word. One of the comments I heard often included this thought, "We are so glad to get some back to the Bible preaching. We are tired of hearing nothing but civil rights, social issues and national and world affairs from the pulpit."

I had never experienced a group of Christians who knew so little about the Bible and the meaning of Christian living. The people of this church asked me if I would accept a full call and continue as the pastor of their church. It sounded good to me, partly because my denomination had given no indication that I would be called to another church in the near future, and also partly because I wanted to stay in pastoral ministry.

Can you believe it?

Yes, I did want to continue in pastoral ministry. I was not sadistically trying to become a martyr. I was not looking for someone else to beat me up. I was not even looking for an easy next church. But I could not shake the idea that I belonged in the pulpit.

I had no choice. God had called me to serve Him as a church pastor. The "call" to serve in the church that requested me to fill their pulpit full time seemed like the Lord's next plan for me and I felt good about this logical consequence.

Before details could be worked out so I could accept the call they wanted to issue, their conference superintendent learned of the plan. He reminded them that established rules forbid them to issue a call to an interim pastor.

The congregation decided they would be wise to keep peace with their superintendent, and, with an apology, did not issue that call.

That superintendent, however, phoned me to say he would be happy to offer me another church, but I would have to transfer my ordination.

Because I wanted to stay in pastoral ministry, I began the process. I completed the paper work and wrote the required paper. All that remained was the interview with their denomination's pastoral board when a phone call came from my own denomination, offering me Church "I".

During those months of waiting for a church to issue me a call, I was aware of a church of my denomination, only a few miles away, conducting their search for a pastor. Why they did not contact me remains a mystery to me. Did they choose not to even give me, as the cliché goes, the "time of day", or had the superintendent discouraged any interest they may have had. I never asked about their "disinterest" in me during the time of uncertainty for me and my wife, but twice, later, after retirement, I served as that church's 18-month interim pastor and they were very complimentary of my ministry and my sermons.

I guess I must leave the "whys" with the Sovereignty of God, though I'm human enough to be tempted to dwell on the fickleness of man. I still ponder why I had to struggle with the misgivings about my ability to fulfill God's call upon my life while not in the pulpit. Perhaps, though, a call to the church that seemed to be ignoring my plight would have interfered with what God had in store for us in Church I.

I was about to find out that Church "I" and I had something in common right from the start.

Church "I"

Coming to Church "I", I soon realized they had been unable to get any other pastor to show any interest in coming there. Is not the Sovereignty of God humbling, amazing, and mysterious, all at the same time? We, this Church and I, needed each other, though I would not see it as easily as the Lord did. After all, I was an experienced pastor, and, is not the world's business model to keep climbing up the ladder of success to bigger and better positions and salaries?

Yes, even we pastors, can become roped into, not only ignoring what we ourselves studied and preached, but also into listening to the wrong coach. If I had not been so depressed from years of cruel words and actions by people also claiming to be God's people, I surely could have reasoned with greater spiritual soundness. Depression can, and did in my case, keep me from realizing I was wrestling blindfolded against the very enemy of God who was continually watching for a sign of my weakness so he could shoot another fiery dart to render me less effective.

Theologically, of course, as a saved pastor, or as a "Blood bought' anyone, the enemy would not win the battle over my soul. But God's enemy was doing that "prowling around looking for someone to devour" written about in I Peter 5:8. You would think that we pastors would realize that if Peter, who was one of those most deeply in fellowship with the Son of God, could write about the devil trying to devour Christ's followers, we would be more intentional about spotting his early attacks and find a way to prevent him any further victories. But God's enemy is subtle, relentless, and he patiently, doggedly, watches for us to reveal our weakness so he can do his devilish work. If Peter, one of the closest friends of our Lord, had to be concerned, who are we to think we are somehow super-Christians and exempt from succumbing to the Lord's number one enemy.

Disciple/Apostle Peter wrote about the tactics of God's enemy, and that same enemy that threatened and longed to crush the earliest believers was also on my case more than I realized. It is his goal to prevent the unsaved from coming to the Lord, so it stands to reason he wanted me kept from preaching, just as he wants other proclaimers of the Gospel silenced or their hearers kept from considering Biblical truth. His second greatest goal is to discourage and discredit those who are already the Lord's, hoping, again, to make the Gospel less palatable to onlookers or would-be converts.

In my case, though I belonged securely to the Lord, the enemy was strategically alert to take advantage of any opportunity to discourage and redirect my thoughts and actions so I would be less effective in serving the Savior I still loved, and Who still loved me and claimed me to be His vessel of Truth. Because I had experienced years of depression without getting "ahead" of it, I was prodded to look back while also trying to look up and firmly take the Lord's hand, and stand steadfastly aware of God's sufficiency and grace.

God, of course, never forgot about me, never cast me aside as worthless even though I was often sure I must be.

God did not, does not, and will not have us "skip school", but for me, then, the Bible had become a book of sermon texts and study lessons. My own love for the Word as a personal guide had dwindled. Now, as I write, my personal love for God's Word has rekindled. Graciously, God moves us believers toward maturity as He works through circumstances and time in His Word to teach us more about His perspective on the time and opportunities He allots us for our earthly lives. God had not forgotten me, and I was, and am now, still "in school" as the situations I encounter come to coax me toward seeing things from God's perspective.

I am aware, and I hope others realize it is true for them as well, that full spiritual maturity and perfectly possessing the mind of Christ does not happen until we are among the throng surrounding the throne. Until then, for better or worse, should we not seek to be as faithful as we know how?

The congregation at "Church I" was happy. They had a full-time pastor and that made them very happy. They were very good to me in every way.

They were so very happy to have me there and I was happy about it as well. I was preaching and fulfilling my desire to be in full-time ministry, which made me happy to have a church, but it did not lift my spirit. After nearly 40 years of pastoral ministry I was now serving the smallest church I had ever served, with the lowest financial support I had ever received (inflation figures taken into consideration) and living in the poorest parsonage of any time in my ministry. Adding to that, I had been accustomed to being invited to preach and give workshops in other churches and be the director, speaker or Bible teacher at Bible Camps every summer of my ministry. Those things did not happen anymore, casting my spirit even lower.

Past experiences continued to weigh heavy on me. Coming to this church really did not help that a bit, but it was so very good to be with a congregation who wanted me and appreciated my ministry.

How is that for a 58-year-old pastor with nearly 40 years of pastoral experience?

Concluding my ministry in such conditions was not the problem. May the reader understand: I would have been quite content with that under other circumstances, but the problem here was what had brought me to this place, that I had been forced into this situation because of my reputation of having made trouble and no other church would show interest.

Incidentally, if you are part of a congregation seeking a pastor, do not adopt the mindset that a 58-year-old pastor is past his prime or that it takes a young pastor to reach young people. I have yet to see that it really works that way. After several months in Church "I", church members told me, "We will never again call a young pastor."

Yes, the people in the church were good to us. Grateful to have a full time pastor again, they were very good to me in every way. They would tell you I had a good ministry there, but in my eyes, I did not.

I had arrived emotionally destroyed, making me unable to be what a pastor ought to be. My preaching continued good, even though I put a lot of wear on the carpet, as I had in Church "G" where I had tried to break the shackles that kept me from getting out to my people.

It is easy to blame others for my condition, but I will have to take the blame myself. I have failed. I have let God down as a pastor.

Eventually I would decide to retire early, based partly upon the circumstances arising from a confrontation with a church leader.

Church "I" was in a "Drinking Town". A few times I had said some things about total abstinence and that I had never known a teetotaler who became an alcoholic.

One church leader's brother owned and managed the local liquor store and at least one of her sons was an alcoholic. Every few months, or so, he would disappear for a few days while on a binge. My remarks offended her, prompting her to tell me, in no uncertain terms, "With your training and your experience with people, you should know that alcoholism is inherited." She defended her alcoholic son by pointing out relatives who have the same problem, claiming, "My son is alcoholic because it is inherited."

I guess she assumed everyone drinks and if the weakness toward alcoholism is in one's genes, alcoholism will result. That's life. My experience in counseling alcoholics was that the control over alcoholism begins once the person realizes that hiding behind the excuse of the genes is futile and the alcoholic discovers he can, through the power of God, gain victory over the control of drink.

After six years, burned out, tired, defeated and feeling I was not giving this church the service a good pastor would give, based upon what I had been able to do earlier in my ministry, I took an early retirement at age 62.

Did I at any time seek professional counseling?

No, I did not. Not yet. Why not?

This was my reasoning that kept me from seeking counseling for my own depression at that point: I had been a psychology major in college. I thought that major would be very helpful in my ministry through the years. And it was, very much so. I saw no problem with psychology and Christian faith working together, but I maintain that counseling in the hands of an unchristian counselor can be a dangerous thing. Through inquiries with denominational leaders and other pastors, I could not find a counselor whom I felt would understand my faith and my problems brought on me by other Christians.

So, with emotional problems still plaguing me, my wife and I again moved back to re-settle in our hometown. I hoped retirement would heal my broken spirit. At least God would not be able to hold me accountable for failing as a church pastor and I would be free from self-condemnation because of more failures as a pastor.

Points to Ponder before We Proceed

1. When you are faced with emotional turmoil, or other problems that arise from unresolved conflict, what is your reaction toward yourself, toward others, and toward the spiritual realm of your life? What steps do you intentionally take toward restoration to wholeness and health?

2. Those who struggle with depression often admit they are unable to benefit from times in prayer or doing Bible study, even if they "know" the Bible holds "life" and "healing" for them. What might be some reasons that would seem to be true?

3. Often those experiencing depression's grip have difficulty seeking "reliable" help, especially help that is Biblically consistent. Why is Biblically consistent help important and what dangers do you think could arise from seeking help from those without an understanding of Biblical truths?

4. If you could have stepped into "Rev's" life during these two pastorates, or if you have a friend feeling similarly defeated, what Bible verses and Biblical counsel would you have wanted to give, and why? What other counsel or actions would you offer?

For Personal Consideration by the Brave-hearted and Obedient:

5. Read and meditate upon or discuss 1 Peter 5: 8-10 (*below*) to pick out the Biblical advice it contains. What admonitions, encouragement or hope does this passage offer to you?

"Be self-controlled and alert. Your enemy the devil prowls around like a roaring lion looking for someone to devour. Resist him, standing firm in the faith, because you know that your brothers throughout the world are undergoing the same kind of sufferings.

"And the God of all grace, who called you to his eternal glory in Christ, after you have suffered a little while, will himself restore you and make you strong, firm and steadfast."

6. Perhaps depression is not something you experience, but few believers sail along without some hindrance to living a life in perfect compliance with the will of God. What nags at you, condemning you from living a life you see as fully pleasing to God? Is the nagging justified or is it a false charge against you? Grace doesn't excuse our sinfulness, but it also emphasizes Christ's love for us even though we are flawed believers with a heart desiring to serve Him more faithfully. What attitude or behavior do you think you need to change to enjoy God's gracious love for you more completely?

7. Where are you in your understanding between living a life fully obedient to the Lord and an attitude of needing to please Him by your works? Jesus said if we love Him, we will obey Him, When are we guilty of hurling ourselves further down into the pit by blindly ignoring the fact that He knows our heart's motives far more than we know His grace.

For pastors in similar circumstances:

8. Read and meditate upon the book of James, this time for counsel to you rather than for the congregation, even though if "Rev's" congregations had applied this book's messages, his pastorate would have gone differently.

Consider that in chapters 1-2, James believes trials are to be joyfully endured and that faith without works is an oxymoron.

In 3, James boldly warns that teachers will be judged more sternly and against harboring bitter envy and selfish ambition.

In 4, James rather harshly speaks of internal battles, advising how to resist the devil and enjoy God's grace while actively living for the Lord.

In 5, James encourages patience in suffering, singing by those happy, prayers of the faithful and the restoration of those straying from truth, not necessary practicing in terms of actions, but in being saturated with Biblical truth.

What benefit is the book of James for those in full time ministry today?

CHAPTER 8:

Steps Along My Road to Recovery

No two people see life the same way and it would be presumptuous of me to assume that your pastor, you, or that friend you want to encourage will be "cured" of past depression by applying what I offer in this chapter. However, I offer these thoughts, hoping lessons I have learned will benefit others, sparing them some of the missteps I made during my bouts with depression. The Holy Spirit might reveal even more or better ways for you.

First, even as a Christian, if the enemy of our Lord and Savior Jesus Christ is pulling you down into a pit, find a trustworthy Christian who will walk with you during this battle. For me, the best solution came from a Christian physician who had both physical knowledge and spiritual armor to help me survive the battle and who could convincingly assure me that we were on the winning team.

I cannot say my physician friend and I have totally slain the persistent enemy. Oh, how I wish the victories we have experienced could spare me, and you, further battles with the deceitful one, but of course, that is not so. As long as I live, I will continue to learn that the Christian's walk is a daily walk of reliance upon the Lord Jesus Christ. The Christian's life will always be the target of the enemy and we would be foolish to think we can live a day without expecting an attack from the enemy, but even more foolish to think we can take on the enemy alone.

The sly enemy remembers my weakest spots. His resources are numerous. Even while I think I am finally wiser, the enemy is plotting a fresh attack. How beneficial for me to realize the enemy can only be defeated by the Lamb of God. Some days I may still need my counseling friend to remind me that the Warrior Jesus Christ, the One who went eye-to-eye with the enemy in the wilderness, Who resolutely and furiously turned the tables over in the temple, Who willingly sacrificed Himself for the defeat of sin and death, is ready to do battle for me (I John 2:1).

The devil is a tough and mean character whose final death will come from the Lord Jesus Himself. He embodies evil and either plots to prevent sinners from recognizing their need of Jesus Christ or he nips at the lives of the redeemed, hoping to cause them discouragement and defeat so that fewer are glorifying God through Jesus Christ. Acknowledging my ongoing propensity to sympathize with those who end up defeated, losers, I cannot but wonder if, momentarily, I will entertain regret that even the evil one, who helped trick millions of souls into a Christ-less eternity, was never humble enough to own up to his sin, repent of his dastardly ways and forsake evil. However, my soul eagerly longs for the indescribably joyful day when all evil is removed forever from the midst of the redeemed.

If you suspect your pastor is depressed, pray that he finds the counselor friend he needs as he climbs out of the pit. Unless your congregation is different from all others, it would be difficult for the depressed pastor to find help among those who are set on criticizing him.

I tried to open up to a few men within my congregations, and some of them would quote scriptures to me. I felt they thought my faith was faltering, that if I had stronger faith, my depression would flee. I suspected they thought their pastor should never be so "spiritually weak" as to be depressed. Perhaps that was not their heart's intention, but it came across to me that way, and it reminded me that in my counseling, a person likely would need more than a scripture I shared.

Christians *can* become depressed. I have ministered to many of them.

There is a saying, "If life hands you lemons, make lemonade." Just like that, eh? I'll tell you, it's not that simple. Besides, lemonade is sour. Why would I want to turn one sour experience into another? You can add sugar to cover up some of the sourness, but it is still there.

Some would say, "Get over it," or "Perk up and smile." That's like telling a person with broken legs to get up and walk it off.

The "holy" people would tell me, "You have to forgive and get it off your chest." They were right, part way. I did have to forgive those who wronged me and I had to let go of bitter memories, but getting depression off my chest and dealing with other consequences of pastoral abuse was not as simple as taking off a tie.

One consequence we pastors can experience after we tell a parishioner about our depression or other problems is conscientious avoidance. If the ones we tell don't have "answers", perhaps because they don't want reminders of their own inadequacy to "solve" problems, they purposefully pull back at a time when the pastor needs a friend. Opening up to someone and telling about your troubles does not mean you expect answers.

During those failed attempts to deal with my depression while serving my churches, I continued to live with my depression. In every church I served there were special people who gave emotional support and encouragement. Even in churches "E" and "G" God raised up those who stayed by my side.

Consequently, I never really quit blaming myself. I easily assumed responsibility for anything that went wrong, and I could never release the memory of those individuals whose words and actions left me feeling abused.

I reminded myself of counseling I had conducted with alcoholics who wanted to excuse alcoholism by saying it was in "the genes". We made no progress in counseling until the alcoholic admitted he was an alcoholic because he drank. Once he admitted his responsibility for drinking, we were on the road toward victory.

Learning How and Why We Can Forgive

In every church I served there were special people who gave emotional support and encouragement. Even in churches "E" and "G" God raised up those who stayed by my side.

I heard an interview on TV where a man asked, "How can I forgive someone who has so drastically changed my life?" Because of an auto crash caused by a drunk driver, the man now lives in constant pain, is permanently handicapped, and grieves the loss of a friend.

I felt as if the man were asking the question I had been trying to answer for so many years. How could I truly forgive those who had so drastically changed my life? Even now, I often ask myself three questions:

"Have I genuinely forgiven them?"

"Am I now forgiving?"

"Do I have a forgiving spirit?"

Perhaps you can recall the news we heard of the stranger who walked into the Amish classroom in Pennsylvania and shot several children to death. The parents of those children said they forgave the gunman, because, after all, that is the duty of Christians.

Please understand I do not doubt the genuineness of these parents. If I remember correctly, they acted out their forgiveness toward their children's slayer. However, my point is that it is much easier to say we forgive because it is the right thing to do than it is to express genuine forgiveness toward our offenders.

Bottom line, genuine forgiveness is a heart condition dependent upon a change brought about by the Holy Spirit because of the Lord Jesus Christ.

I do not really expect anyone who has not had similar experiences to understand what I am about to write, but I prayerfully hope these words will help you understand, support and encourage those dealing with hurt and depression caused by the hold others have on their lives.

In a nutshell, here is the truth: By being a forgiving person, you might well save your own sanity. However, once we forgive, we are wise to realize the task of forgetting is not magically complete. My experience has been that consequences of the emotional damage can very well linger.

No, that is not fair.

Yes, those consequences leave the abused or offended with an unwelcome burden that can become part of their "cross" as they mature: Though few will ever totally forget the offenses committed against them, choosing to forgive means loss of the "right" to bring the matter up again. We "forgivers" lose the right to continue condemning those who offended us.

Because we are not good "forgetters", we may "need" to recall the destructive actions and words that have hindered us so that we continue with our healing, or in this case, with the hopes that others can be spared similar destruction. But as those who desire to be forgiving, we recall without condemnation, and our own blood pressure, our own mind can quickly gauge whether we have forgiven others as we write or speak of past abuse toward us.

As I deal with memories still insistent upon sharing hours of my retirement, I pray my heart is generally such that I can assuredly say, "I do forgive," and "I have forgiven."

I forgive because I have been forgiven. The One Who continually forgives my sin places His Spirit within my heart, causing me to imitate Him, to be forgiving toward others.

Though I agree not to bring up the old abuses again in ways that let them fester and do harm, I acknowledge the scars left behind.

At one time, I sat in a pew with heart, soul and mind loaded with scars and listened to a sermon on turning all your past, all your terrible experiences and all those bad memories over to Jesus. I sat through the entire sermon agreeing with him, but also thinking, "That's easy for you to say," and, "How do you do that when your scars are haunting you daily?"

The pastor gave a few words about Jesus, who He is and what He has promised, but by that time, I was lost in the memories of the past. When I was a little boy on the farm, I stuck my hand in where it should not have been. Until I get my glorified body, my right hand will remain badly scarred, an ever present reminder of that day in my childhood. It doesn't matter where I am or what I am doing, the scars are on my right hand are always within.

Most of my emotional scars are like that, and I have multiple reasons to believe they will remain for other scarred people, too.

The Amish parents now live their lives without their children, finding comfort in their faith and in good memories of earlier times with those precious young ones before they experienced the consequences of the gunman's evil action. I, too, forgive my offenders, I forgive myself for inadequately handling abusive behavior toward me, and I continue to live my life with memories of experiences I would not have readily chosen.

God in His Sovereignty, however, allowed those experiences to fall into the pathway of my life, and so I write, not to complain, not to seek self-pity or point fingers, but in the hope of correcting some wrong opinions and wrong practices and in the hope of sparing others similar unnecessary experiences. Revealing the consequences of my emotional abuse can possibly stop some of the emotional abuse inflicted upon pastors, and others, by church attendees.

One test of forgiveness would be this: Can I walk up to the offender and give a firm hug? Remembering wrongs, harboring bitterness toward an offender, won't prevent the offender from going his merry way, but it will slowly kill us who are slow to forgive.

Bear in mind that whether or not the offending person has asked for forgiveness has nothing to do with one's own spirit of forgiveness. I will say it again, I pray that I, and you dear reader, will live in a spirit of forgiveness even though the person(s) offending us have not asked for forgiveness.

Forgiveness brings many benefits to the "forgiver". Isn't that just like God? He showers us with unexpected benefits as He remakes our minds and hearts so they are more like His Son's. Remember this, be quick to forgive, for your own sake as well as for the bridge it can build to those you forgive.

Helpers in Human Flesh

Overcoming depression cannot be done alone. Such a person definitely needs the Lord, but he also needs persons in the flesh.

There were times my thoughts wandered to the young intern pastor who served with me as my Assistant back at Church G before most of the troubles began. One day, now in my retirement, I sent him an email message. He responded by filling me in on his family and his ministry while inquiring about my family.

I wrote him about our family and then I unloaded a portion of my burdens.

It was an encouragement to me that he did not ignore my letters, and more exchanges followed. Finally, I apologized to him, explaining my original intent had simply been to renew our friendship, not to dump my troubles upon him. I thanked him for hearing me.

Just having a friend with whom to correspond was special.

Later, sitting in the examination room of my Christian physician, I asked if I might be a candidate for antidepressant medication.

He spoke of his admiration for me and my ministry even in retirement before inquiring about my history or asking why I felt I might need an anti-depressant.

I told him about my depression and some of the history behind it.

I repeat what he said because I want you to hear it again. He told me he counsels and mentors a number of pastors who have been through very similar experiences, adding, "Without a doubt, being a pastor is the most difficult job in all the world."

I agree, and I also ask, "Why is it so?" Pastors are surrounded by and working with Christians, a word that means "Christ Ones".

So why is the pastor's job so difficult? Could it be because so much of the time Christians are not very Christ-like? I recall reading one author who wrote, "The problem with the church is that its members have a faith that does not transform them into being Christ-like".

On the follow-up visit to check on the effects of the medication my physician said, "Let's have breakfast together some morning. How about Saturday?"

That breakfast turned into a three-hour meeting. After talking about my life history since childhood this question came, "What did God the Father say to his Son at the baptism?"

I answered, "You are my Beloved Son in whom I am well pleased."

"Say it again."

And I did.

"Say it again."

And I did.

This went on for eight or 10 times while I'm thinking, "But this was God the Father speaking to His Son Jesus, and I'm not Jesus."

The next morning, I was lying on the couch while those words, kept surfacing in my mind. My mind went back to, "But this was God the Father speaking to His Son Jesus, and I'm not Jesus."

My physician had spoken of how the devil likes to use situations like this as an opportunity to use his wiles. I recognized my thoughts as coming from the devil so I sat up and blurted out in loud words, "Satan, you old devil, in the name of Jesus Christ I command you to leave me alone."

Dear Christian friends, Satan has more to do with our troubles than we realize. We need to recognize this and send him on his way. He is totally helpless in the presence or even the mention of Jesus Christ.

In my earlier years of ministry I would on occasion command Satan to get out of here in the name of Jesus Christ! I did it in an audible voice because he cannot read minds. Only members of the Trinity can do that.

How did I get away from doing that? Had Satan kept me from recognizing his dirty work?

My physician reminded me of Satan's dirty tricks.

I have renewed the practice of speaking loudly to that deceiver. I have told my wife that if she hears me call out loudly from my office, "Get out of here. Leave me alone!." I am not yelling at her.

If you or your loved one or pastor is dealing with depression, recognize that person's need for a wise Christian friend who is comfortable recognizing that the enemy of God is alive and active and must be commanded, in the name of Jesus Christ, to depart.

Dear Christian friends, we need to recognize the presence of Satan in this world. In Holy Scripture he is called the "prince of this world" (John 12:31, 14:30, 16:11, II Cor. 4:4) and the prince of the power of the air (Eph. 2:2). Satan is sly and deceptive in the way he does his work (II Cor. 11:14, Rev. 12:9). We need to recognize this, but we also need to recognize that he is totally helpless in the presence of, or even the mention of the name of Jesus Christ.

We need have no fear of the devil. He was defeated at the cross. God has allowed him to hang around, but he is on a tether. God holds the tether and controls its length. Our place is to place full faith in God and "Be self-controlled and alert. Your enemy the devil prowls around like a roaring lion looking for someone to devour. Resist him, standing firm in the faith, because you know that your brothers throughout the world are undergoing the same kind of sufferings." (I Peter 5:8, 9)

Our God has the power over the devil. Our part is to recognize God's power and submit to God as the Ruler of our thoughts, plans and actions.

In speaking of the devil, I will offer this advice: Do not be so focused on getting the devil out that you lose your focus on Jesus Christ. A youth camp where I was the speaker and Bible teacher began on Sunday evening. By Monday evening, a counselor cried out, "The devil is in this camp. We've got to get rid of the devil."

His cries continued throughout Tuesday. At the staff's Wednesday morning prayer meeting, I said, "I'm sure the devil is enjoying all the attention he is getting. He has been getting credit for his control over this camp and he likes that. Let us turn our attention off of the devil and concentrate on Jesus Christ Who has power over the devil."

At that point, the mood of the staff changed, as did the mood of the entire camp. Through the remainder of the week, several young people accepted Jesus Christ as personal Savior and Lord and the faith of others was revived.

I encourage you to read Romans 6 and 8, giving special attention to verses 28-39 at the end of chapter 8.

On the cross, God disarmed all the power of the devil (Col. 2:15).

Do not worry about him, just "Submit your-selves, then, to God. Resist the devil and he will flee from you" (James 4:7).

Yes, the devil is still hanging around even though he knows he is the looser and Christ the Victor. Do not mess around with a loser.

Yes, the devil is real in this world, and I know there is a time for exorcism. Exorcism is a spiritual gift given by the Holy Spirit to selected Christians. May we resist the devil long before we need exorcism by walking in the newness of life through Jesus Christ (James 4:7; Romans 6:4).

Additional Strength within the Scriptures

I cannot leave this portion of my writing without passing along two scriptures that have greatly benefitted me during my steps toward re-establishing a closer fellowship with God through His written Word. I meditated upon them with the hope of restoring my trust in God's Word. During those years of the depth of my depression I fell far behind in the reading of His Word. I lost my love for God's Word. I continued reading, somewhat, but it was like a chore that had to be done.

Just as sometimes a person needs to "start over" physically by re-learning how to walk or talk after a debilitating accident or illness, I discovered I had to re-learn how to rest upon God's precious promises.

These scripture portions are becoming increasingly precious to me as I make progress in my own recovery. God's Word is forever new, ministering to us "where we are" even if we have walked with God for decades. It truly is God's "living" word.

There is Romans 8:28, "We know that all things work together for good to them that love God, to them who are the called according to his purpose." Can I believe that and put my trust fully in those words? Or, are they just some of those lovely sentiments we love to quote at difficult times? I am re-learning how to believe with confidence the declaration within this sacred passage.

Another healing passage is Psalm 34:15, 17: "The eyes of the Lord are upon the righteous, and His eyes are open unto their cry . . . The righteous cry, and the Lord hears and delivers them out of all their troubles." Again, is that really true? I am re-learning how to live that belief that God sees and hears me and works toward my deliverance. When those truths totally sink in, when they become like spiritual anchors, I know I will be again overwhelmed with the love God has for me, just as you, or others, can become overwhelmed by His love for you. I am confident He loves me now, but I know I have not come close to apprehending the fullness of His love.

The Lord is eager to direct His children to "food" for their souls in His Word. Perhaps you have known loved ones who were struggling with a physical illness and had no desire to eat or drink what would help restore them. Similarly, I would encourage any depressed person to keep nibbling at the "Food" even when it does not seem appealing, because it does bring healing by the Great Physician.

Is This Victory I Am Feeling?

I am forgiven and forgiving.

My long journey has now brought me to that road marker which has me realizing, praise the Lord, that not only am I forgiven, but that I have forgiven and am forgiving.

You can get to that part of the road, too.

There comes a time when you quit struggling and wake up to the truth that the Lord has covered it all. The cleansing has taken place. It is finished.

When you or I are in an emotionally disturbed condition, it takes time for this to strike home even though in your head you know it to be true.

There then comes the time when you quit praying to be released from the thorn because the truth finally soaks in: I am already released in Christ's finished work. It is true as Miles Stanford writes, "In most cases of appropriation, there is a waiting period between the acceptance and the receiving – often of years." ("The Complete Green Letters").

All who carry scars of emotional abuse will begin experiencing a quiet and abiding joy the day they awake and realize the grace and forgiveness has settled into the corners of their hearts and minds. The sooner that day arrives, the better for the individual experiencing that realization, and the better for those to whom they minister.

My Prayer

I pray for each of you who read of my experiences, experiences with which many of you can identify. I pray that you will show kindness and consideration to all people, especially your pastor and other members of your church.

Read, please, and meditate upon I Timothy 5:17. "The elders who direct the affairs of the church well are worthy of double honor, especially those whose work is preaching and teaching".

I pray that you will put an end to all criticism while recognizing that even criticism intended to be constructive can come across as rejection. Do not think your words are constructive and edifying just because you think they are. Even if the other person understands that your words are intended to be constructive and edifying, they still hurt.

At the first chapter of this book I mentioned those who go on shooting sprees and those who commit suicide. I do, of course, feel deep sympathy for the families of these victims, but my heart really goes out to the ones who committed the terrible deeds. There is a common denominator in almost every case. Something in their experiences brought them to this point in life. That something was criticism (failure to be accepted, i.e. rejection, is a form of criticism) and a lack of support and encouragement.

These perpetrators are probably not happy. They have very few friends, if any. If they have a friend, that person has probably been a bad influence. They might be moody and quiet. They have been sending out signals all along, signals that no one interpreted.

In my thinking, I am always in defense of those who have been charged with a crime. My friends can't understand how I can do that, "They are guilty" they say. We don't know that, I say, but even if found guilty, there is still a person there, a human being with a living soul whom God loves. My heart goes out to him as I think of what his life must have been like to bring him to this point in life and what his life could have been like. When we look into the lives of these people, we often find that there has been someone, or some group, who had a negative influence on those poor souls. It was preventable. Let us live for those around us, even the strangers. Make it your goal to make others happy. Ask yourself, "Are those I meet any better because of having known me?"

Those shootings at Columbine, Von Maur and the Amish school should never have been had the perpetrators' families, friends and even acquaintances picked up on what was brewing inside those people. Many realized it later, but it was too late. These people might well be living with a terrible sense of guilt as they think of what could have been. So be a friend and an encourager to all people before they get to where they show signs of emotional disturbance.

Finally, check your criticisms. Even if you criticize behind their backs, you are damaging someone, even if only yourself.

Whenever I hear of someone going on a shooting spree, I hold back the tears and say, "I'm so sorry dear friend. I understand". Whenever I hear of someone committing suicide, I hold back the tears and say, "I'm so sorry, dear friend. I understand". With the treatments I got, but for the grace of God, I could easily have been in your shoes.

Maybe there is one near you who is not happy with the way his life is. Be a friend and hand out compliments and encouragement.

Maybe there is one near you who just heard some discouraging words from his boss. He could use a hug and a friend who will shed a few tears with him. I have had funerals where I cried along with the family. Later these people usually told me of what a comfort they felt to have their pastor cry with them.

Many living on the down side of life need you to be a "lifter", a Barnabas. I found it difficult to get singers to come with me to do worship services in nursing homes, a missed opportunity. I found it difficult to get anyone, even pastors, to come with me, or take a turn, to do a service at the jail or at the mental institution. More missed opportunities.

The list can go on. The troubled people are not difficult to find. As a believer in Jesus Christ, you always have the Good News of the Gospel of Jesus Christ to share, but do it at the right time in a loving and tactful way. No preaching. In James 1:27 we read, "Religion that God our father accepts as pure and faultless is this: to look after orphans and widows in their distress and to keep oneself from being polluted by the world." I am sure James had more than widows and orphans in mind ad he wrote those words.

I shall always remember a young man I met along my years of ministry. I first met him at Bible Camp. I was the speaker. He was a counselor. My first impression of him was, "My goodness. Are we that desperate that we have to scrape the bottom of the barrel to get counselors?" A victim of an earlier disease he literally stumbled along as he walked and he spoke very haltingly as he curled his mouth into contortions in order to get the right words out.

During the week I observed him as he gave a thrilling testimony of his walk with the Lord, the boys in his cabin had the greatest of love and respect for him. By the end of the week, he had led several boys in his group to personal faith in the Savior. I invited him to come to my church and speak to our people. When he was asked how he can live alone and do his own cooking he said, "Well, I drop an egg into the skillet and then I pick out the shells." But those of his words which I'll never forget; I can visualize him stumbling as he walked and stammering as he spoke while saying, "I'm glad God made me this way because now I can understand those people who are stricken by crippling diseases and accidents." But please do not think that not being crippled does not mean you can't reach out to the crippled. And please do not think that having not been criticized you can't reach out to those who have been or are being criticized.

Always show kindness to all people at all times

Think about this: the way you speak to and the way you treat another person has far reaching effects, probably much more than you realize. Think about it again; the way you speak to and the way you treat another person has deep effect. You the reader, yes you, are an influence in shaping the people with whom you have contact every day. Just think of the power you have. Someone could well go far and contribute much to the Lord's work, to the nation and to the community because of something you said. You might not know it for years or at all, but your words are doing their thing. Words are like feathers freed in the wind from a broken pillow. They can never be retrieved. Be sure they are words well spoken. Proverbs 25:11 says, "A word aptly spoken is like apples of gold in a setting of silver". No one ever got to where he is alone, whether a good person or a bad person. He got there surrounded by people: church people, class mates, teachers, neighbors, store clerks, restaurant waiters and waitresses and the list can go on.

Understand people – all people. I was told about a high school class reunion. One member of the class did not come to the reunion, but sent a note in response to the invitation. He wrote, "You showed no interest in me back in high school so why would you want me to come now?"

Some said, "Well, what did he expect?" The blame was heaped upon the absent member of the class, with claims that the absent member had never shown any interest in them and had not encouraged anyone to be his friend. No one defended him.

His classmates missed the opportunity to be a friend during the years of school together.

Had he outgrown their rejection? Obviously not. He was still carrying that burden of rejection after all these years. He revealed that he had wanted friends, that he did not like being a loner. Yes, pride can make people shy, but sensing rejection can cause a person to withdraw into a self-preservation mode. That classmate needed someone brave enough to step out and investigate the possibility of a friendship. Too bad they learned it late if at all.

In Galatians 6:10 we read, "Therefore, as we have opportunity, let us do good to all people, especially to those who are of the family of believers." I fear that Christians are no better at living by this than the people of the world are. The people of the world, such as business people, practice this because they know its effect. We Christians have it right there before us in God's Holy Scripture.

Then I repeat this verse; I Tim. 5:17, "The elders who direct the affairs of the church well are worthy of double honor, especially those whose work is preaching and teaching." Don't get hung up on that word "well". Church leaders are human and will make some mistakes while still doing the work well. That's where your forgiving spirit must reign. There are also differences in talents and Spiritual Gifts. Some are strong in preaching and teaching, but not so strong in other areas. Some are born administrators while others are terrible at this.

Be a friend. Show a lot of kindness to everyone at all times. Let me illustrate from the animal world. As a boy on the farm, I loved animals. When I became a teenager I was known in the neighborhood as the one who could handle cantankerous horses. I was helping one man round up his horses on a Monday morning. On weeknights they would be kept in a fenced in area, but on Saturday night they were put out to pasture. Bringing them to the barn on Monday morning was a difficult job to say the least. The gate was in the corner of the pasture, but the horses would circle around and not go near it. Then my friend got his pickup and tried to chase them through the gate that way, but the pickup could not maneuver as well as a horse so he gave that up and went back to chasing them on foot. When he became angry, puffing, sweating and red in the face, I told him to sit down under a tree and rest a while. "I have an idea". I went to the barn for a halter. I came back and walked slowly up to one of the horses, these were pulling contest champions, each of whom weighed a ton. Patting the horse on his neck and stroking his nose I slipped the halter on. As I lead that horse to the barn the other followed thinking, I suppose, "We're a team. We belong together". If animals will respond like that to kindness, what about people who think, have feelings and emotions?

Spend much time in prayer before you speak. Do not criticize or speak negatively about anyone or anything that you cannot take to the Lord and pray about before you say anything. Examine your motives for wanting to intervene. Be very sure you are listening to what the Lord is saying to you. Take it to the Lord and then do what needs to be done and say what needs to be said.

Take it to the Lord and if He says "Drop the matter", then drop it.

A word of caution must be given. Never say, "The Lord told me to say it" if the Lord did not tell you to say it, no matter how strongly you think the Lord told you to say it. It is easy to get your own feeling mixed up with the Lord's will. Case in point: A woman phoned my wife one morning and said "I am sorry I hurt the pastor with what I said last night, but the Lord told me to say it." My reaction to my wife was, "The Lord would never direct anyone to speak to another like that". Pray and examine your words before you speak. I suspect the Lord gets unduly credited with more things said by people in church than will ever be justified when every idle and evil word will be reviewed by Him. As the scriptures urge; "Set a guard over my mouth, O Lord; keep watch over the door of my lips" (Psalm 141:3) and "Above all else, guard your heart, for it is the wellspring of life". (Proverbs 4:23)

I pray that you will keep close to the Holy Scriptures and take the Lord at His word. Psalm 51 has been special to me over these years, as has also Psalm 32.

As I read Psalm 51, I can identify with David. No, I have not committed a sin anything at all like the one he committed with Bathsheba, but during my state of depression, I neglected some duties and failed in others. These sins have bothered me a lot, even though I know I am forgiven. In this Psalm, I realize I am in pretty good company for David writes in verse 3, "For I know my transgressions and my sin is always before me". Verses 10-12 are my daily prayer, and verse 17 is special to me because I can identify so closely with, "a broken spirit and a broken and contrite heart".

I encourage you to read Psalm 32 and meditate on those words, but I will here share Verses 1, 3 and 11; "Blessed is he whose transgressions are forgiven, whose sins are covered. Blessed is the man whose sin the Lord does not count against him and in whose spirit there is no deceit. . . . Rejoice in the Lord and be glad, you righteous; sing, all you who are upright in heart!"

I John 2:1, tenderly appeals to me when it says, "My little children, these things I write unto you, that ye sin not. And *if any man sin, we have an advocate with the Father, Jesus Christ the righteous.*" (Italics mine) (KJV) What a precious picture for those of us who know we are sinners dependent upon the sinless Son of God who faithfully pleads our righteousness before God the Father because of His own purity imparted to us. What relief to know that I have the "best

Someone" as my personal advocate. My Advocate never loses a case and none of His clients are ever condemned.

My prayer is that our precious Lord Jesus Christ will give you peace with yourself, with your friends and with Himself.

Points to Ponder

1. Take time to thank the Lord that He forgives your sin, that He is your advocate before the Father if you sin again, that even though you remember your sins, He does not, (Micah 7:19, Psalm 85:2, Jer. 31:34c, Isa. 65:17)

2. Take several minutes to sit in quietness, or walk as some find this the best way to meditate, and think of your fellow church members and other friends and relatives who could really use your friendship and encouragement right now.

3. Try to think of any criticisms or negative thoughts that you might have of someone. Can you humbly bow before the Lord and ask him to remove all such thoughts and give you love to pass on to others?

CHAPTER 9:

Lord, If You're Asking Me to Encourage My Pastor, What Do I Do?

You, my reader, have come a long way with me. Thank you for sticking with the course. I hope you, too, have gained from our time together. Just knowing you are reading my words verifies my experiences were not for me alone and that because I am open about my pastoral abuse, possibly others will be spared some of the scars I carry.

This chapter will offer some review and summarizes some of the thoughts and experiences too often experienced by pastors in our churches.

A depressed person is in no condition to help him-self. A depressed pastor, the spiritual head of the body of believers to whom he has been called, has limited possibilities, partly because either the problem includes relationships within the congregation, or the congregation's expectation of him is that he should not be so "fragile" or "immature" so as to need a counselor himself.

So, to whom does a pastor turn for help? Most pastors too often conclude they have to handle their depression, and other problems, alone because there is no one, no other human, who can offer help. As an alcoholic hides his alcohol as best as he can; so the depressed pastor, out of fear that he will be looked upon as having lost his faith, too often tries to hide his depression as best as he can.

Sooner or later, though, evidence about depression becomes too noticeable to ignore if the pastor does not find constructive ways to handle the churning and turmoil that goes on within his mind and heart. Pastors are, after all, human, too, and may God prevent them from dishonoring Him or harming others if he is left alone to battle depression without assistance from someone who cares.

If your pastor is closer to some church members than others, that is good. He is not playing favorites. Even pastors, and pastor's spouses, need special friends. Pastors' spouses very much feel the brunt of troubles in the church. Be grateful your pastor and family feel comfortable with members of the church, and if you are part of that circle, be willing to be a trusted friend when pressure mounts or when the family experiences "typical life" with its sorrows, heartaches, failures and its triumphs, joys and celebrations.

However, individuals within the church should consider options their pastor may have if he is dealing with a personal crisis like depression.

Other than his wife, the pastor is likely to conclude there is no other shoulder on which he can cry. But dare he cry on his wife's shoulder? He may not want to burden his wife because he wants to protect her from dealing with members' shortcomings or attacks, or he may desire to leave his work at the office so that his home is a safe and peaceful escape from work's pressures. Perhaps he does not confide in his wife for fear she will see him as less manly or less spiritual if he reveals his depression to her, or that she may become fearful that his mental state puts the family's safety at risk.

It is also possible the wife will subconsciously block his attempts to confide in her about his depression. Though she may suspect he needs help, perhaps even wanting to suggest her husband seek help, she may feel safest by "not rocking the boat", adapting the family routines and conversations in hopes of not making her husband less secure. As the wife of a depressed businessman confided, "We all have to walk on eggshells so my husband doesn't become upset." This pastor's wife spent too many years walking on eggshells. Healthy individuals do not want to live that way.

Additionally, the pastor will probably not feel free to open the conversation to those who have been throwing the "stones" because his own heart knows it is beginning to harbor anger, his tongue wants to hurl accusations and he is not certain he will be able to prevent those out-bursts. The pastor intentionally does not want to hinder the Lord's work in his community.

Further, he may be unaware of who can offer skilled help and a listening ear, especially if others have been coming to him for counsel. Why should the counselor need counseling? Well, I guess that is something like asking if a physician can get sick.

He may also be condemning himself, or denying his need for counsel, because, after all, two tactics of the enemy are condemnation and pride. These fiery missiles rush in to tell him he ought to be so spiritual that he is beyond petty things like depression.

He may be unaware he is in the crosshairs of the enemy's weaponry, which delights the enemy who is eager to deliver a crippling blow.

If these are the conditions for your pastor, dear reader, it is up to you to pray diligently for your pastor and simultaneously do all the Lord prompts you to do to encourage your pastor. Yours may be the shoulder he is to cry on if that is what he needs. However, you must be a trustworthy confidant.

If you cannot be an encourager and maintain respect for the leader of your congregation in spite of his depleted emotional state, you are probably not the shoulder he will need.

If you are a female, you are not the shoulder for a male pastor, unless you go with your husband to offer the counsel.

If your pastor is female, a sympathetic male is not who she needs either, unless it is her own husband.

Although your intentions may be pure, the consequences, or the inevitable speculation and suspicion that can arise may only intensify the problem.

I tenderly remember when my chairman and I stood in my office, after a church business meeting where I had been criticized, and cried on each other's shoulders. I suspect other pastors can warmly recall those who shared similar moments in their ministry when someone seemed to truly understand the burdens pastors carry. Sometimes that closeness comes within a close pastoral fellowship group that prays together, but finding pastoral groups that get together for prayer without jealous at the other's success or competing for each other's members can be a challenge. Though created with human frailties like the rest of mankind, pastors seem to somehow be a "strange breed" in many ways. Maybe God calls them, not because of the work He wants them to accomplish with their gifts, but because He knows they need a lot of work by the Holy Spirit and by those obedient to the Holy Spirit before their work will matter one iota for eternity. God is gracious to all, especially to pastors perhaps.

My son's team was playing an away baseball game. The home field people, not aware of the hitting ability of 13 and 14 year old boys, had left a snow fence in place which had been used as the outfield fence for girls' softball. My son was on the mound when a batter hit a long ball which appeared certain to go over the fence. The center fielder jumped high and reached out to catch that ball as it was coming down just over the fence. Catching the ball, that center fielder came down with his ribs crashing on the slats of that snow fence. My first thought was, "It's not bad being a pitcher when you have that kind of dedication behind you." Then, almost immediately, another thought hit me, "It's not bad being a pastor when you have that kind of dedication behind you".

Points to Ponder

The church is a team. Some are on the field while others are on the bench waiting their turn and yet very much a part of the game. Everyone is a member of the team. There are also those in the stands (Hebrews 12:1). Have there been times when the way you handled your position, i.e., the way you used or did not use your spiritual gifts, was a definite help or hindrance to others on the team?

What are some ways that you could use your spiritual gifts to strengthen the ministry of your pastor and others on your team?

Pastors need a Barnabas. Ask yourself, could I be called a "Barnabas"? Barnabas is the name the apostles gave to a certain Joseph because he was so good at giving encouragement.

Let me offer a few questions for your checklist in the following paragraphs. Ask yourself some of these questions, or prayerfully ask the Lord what persons might be qualified to become an encourager to your pastor. I also offer some questions for you to consider when you are too eager to rush to judgment about him.

In recent years, an unusually large number of pastors have joyfully begun their ministry knowing they had a call from God only to give it up in a few years and find another line of work. I offer these paragraphs with gentleness, but with the conviction that more pastors would survive their "call" if these soul-searching questions and paragraphs were considered frequently.

Why do you suppose pastors leave the pastoral ministry while still in the prime of life?

Do I contribute to the making of my pastor, or am I weakening or even extinguishing the light my pastor brings to our congregation?

How do I speak to my pastor?

How do I speak *about* my pastor?

How do I treat my pastor? What effort do I make to be a part of his life during the week?

Take a good look at how you *speak of* him when he is not around.

Are you willing to be a Barnabas? Every church member has a responsibility to encourage and build up others.

Do not worry about making your pastor conceited. God has ways of humbling His children who spend time with Him. Keeping the pastor humble is not our job. You will not find that as one of the Spiritual gifts.

God may be prompting you to be the human who comes along side to be an encourager to your pastor, or to be someone who helps ensure his mental and physical health. Can you answer: Who sees that the pastor gets regular physical check-ups? Is his family able to get the medical care they need, or is this part of the "cross" the church assigns the pastor's family to carry?

Do I give my pastor the benefit of doubt when he seems aloof or abrupt?

When you hear another person criticize your pastor what do you do? Do you join in with some criticism of your own, do you ignore the criticism or do you remind that person that he should be more positive and look at the good points in his pastor? Maybe tell him that if he can't say something good to say nothing at all?

Too well I recall the day, while serving church E, when I drove for ten hours to be back home for a community meeting in the evening. At the meeting, we were divided into smaller groups to discuss some community issue.

The next day, one of my church leaders jumped on me because a member of my group had phoned him to ask, "What's the matter with that pastor of yours? He was just plain uncivil last night."

My church leader immediately took the man's words as truth. I could not believe that anyone would say I was "uncivil". As I remembered that evening I had been quite pleasant and sociable, aside from being extremely tired.

My church leader missed his opportunity to ask, "Were you not feeling well last night?" or "Was something bothering you last night?" He apparently figured we pastors are all super-humans who never need rest and never have an imperfect day.

He heard a rumor, jumped to a conclusion and I became the bad guy.

He, and others, similarly eager to criticize, helped me lose faith in Christians. Those who will encourage their pastor are hard to find. Pastors who are reading these words will immediately, in their own mind, think of many similar experiences. Am I prone to believe negative things I hear about others? Am I willing to sort out the story and get to the truth?

As I lost faith in Christians, I would get upset, and even so to this day whenever I hear people use expressions like "Praise the Lord" or "Hallelujah". Why would those expressions upset me? Because the people in church "E" and again in church "G" who were the center of the criticism and troubles were generous with those words and other "holy sounding" expressions. Take a little time to think about this paragraph and discuss it with friends.

A simple task may be discovering hobbies your pastor has, and who among the congregation or community share enthusiasm for the same hobby. Hobbies help your pastor see measurable accomplishments on days when he may be tempted to think he has nothing to show for his efforts that filled his week. To be able to hold something in your hand and say, "I made this" means a lot to any person's emotions.

However, pastors are not the only ones wanting and needing an encourager.

There are people out there who have been through divorce, are living in a difficult relationship, have recently lost a spouse, had a child killed in an auto accident or dying of a terminal decease, have children who have caused trouble, a son killed in the war, the list can go on. A mother came to our house one evening with her seventh grade son. The boy said the kids at school pick on him. He needed a friend who would indeed be a friend and let him cry his heart out. You can be such a friend. You can be a comforter to those who have such a need and thus be the instrument for emotional healing.

I hear people say, "I would like to go see that person, but I don't know what to say. To that I say, "You don't *have* to say anything." Remember Job? His friends came to see him and they sat with him for seven days and seven nights before they said anything. They were doing just fine at that point, but then they opened their mouths. Their presence was encouraging, but much of their speaking was judgmental. You, of course, would not be judgmental, would you, to someone who has been through difficulty?

There have been times when I was ill or had been injured and people came and said the wrong things. Just two examples: I had deep vein thrombosis (blood clots) in my leg. It gave great pain and I was hospitalized for a few days. There were those who came to me to tell me that "If you had done such and such this would not have happened". Not much comfort there. A friend of mine fell off his roof and broke a hip. There were those who said, "What were you thinking?" and "You had no business being up on that roof." Not much comfort or encouragement there.

Be a good listener. If the hurting person says nothing, be a good "sitter". James writes in his epistle, chapter 1, verse 19, "My dear brothers, Take note of this: Everyone should be quick to listen, slow to speak . . . ". Do not try to pry anything out of anyone. Give him a hug, linger a while and be on your way to return again later.

If you have to admit you are quick to criticize your pastor, or others, it may be necessary to step back to look at yourself.

I remember someone in my childhood church who always found something for which to criticize the pastor each Sunday. He would meet the pastor just before the worship service to deliver his criticism, and then expect the pastor to lead a good worship.

I also have memories of another, a few years later in the same church, who would hit the pastor at the end of the worship hour after he had given a spiritually edifying message from God's Word.

Did it not ever enter these minds that maybe, just maybe, it was they who were wrong?

Certainly there are times when church leaders should sit down with the pastor and have a good "Lay it all on the table" discussion. Choose the place, time, and especially the words very carefully. Check your attitude before meeting. Come not with a chip on your shoulder, but with an open mind ready to listen and change your mind if you must. Moreover, do not have such a confrontational meeting just before or just after the Sunday morning worship time. Try to avoid a Sunday meeting at all if possible. At such a meeting, you need to exercise what Rick Warren calls EGR: Extra Grace Required. I have discovered, and I'm sure you have too, EGR is a good practice at all times.

In Galatians 6:1, 2 we read, "Brothers, if someone is caught in a sin, you who are spiritual should restore him *gently*. But watch yourself, or you may also be tempted. *Carry each other's burdens*, and in this way you will fulfill the law of Christ." (Italics mine) Think about it. Have I contributed to another's burdens? Have I allowed another to share his burdens with me? Also get these words in I Timothy 5:1, 2, "Do not rebuke an older man harshly, but exhort him as if he were your father. Treat younger men as brothers, older women as mothers, and younger women as sisters, with absolute purity." That includes also, maybe especially, pastors, those whose work is to win souls for Christ and to help them grow in their faith.

Consider this: Representatives from a church went to a veteran pastor and asked advice on how they can get rid of their pastor. Here is what he told them:

"Keep telling your pastor what a good job he's doing. Compliment his sermons and speak of how meaningful and helpful they have been. Show him appreciation for his Bible Studies."

"What good will that do? We want to get rid of him."

"You do that and he'll feel so good and get so inspired that he will preach excellent sermons and his studies will get so good that a big church will take him away from you."

They decided to try it, and sure enough, it did become apparent that their encouraging words got him fired up and inspired. His preaching got much better, His Bible

Studies improved. As predicted, he did receive a call from another church, but by that time, the congregation decided they wanted him to stay.

Watch out. Encouraging words change people. Are you ready for it?

If you are the Barnabas God placed within your pastor's congregation, you may not only spare him long bouts with depression, but you both may discover what good friends you can be for each other in spite of your shortcomings.

Your pastor may rediscover an excitement as he digs into the scriptures to prepare for his sermons, and you may find yourself eagerly anticipating how God will use your pastor to help you grow into greater spiritual maturity, largely because you became an encourager.

One has to wonder if you are both closer to fulfilling God's proposed ministry within the Body of Christ on earth.

I pray for each of you who read of my experiences, experiences that can be identified with many pastors. I pray that you will show kindness and consideration to all people, especially your pastor and all the other members of your church. I pray that you will put an end to all criticism that is not constructive and edifying. Don't criticize anyone about anything that you can't take to the Lord and pray about. Take it to the Lord and you'll probably decide it's not that serious in the ongoing life of the church. I have heard a lot of criticism that was called constructive that certainly was not. Again I say; if you must criticize anyone, pray about it first and then listen to the Lord and not your own thoughts.

I pray that you will keep close to the Holy Scriptures and take the Lord at his word. Psalm 51 has been special to me over these years as has also Psalm 32.

I close this section with I John 2:1, a verse that has become special to me as I am recovering, "My dear children, I write to you, so that you will not sin. But, if anybody does sin, we have one who speaks to the Father in our defense - Jesus Christ the Righteous One."

May the Lord Jesus Christ give you peace with yourself, with your friends and especially with Himself.

Here I choose to include a sermon I have given a few times on my last Sunday with a congregation as well as in churches where I was the interim pastor or pulpit supply pastor.

CHAPTER 10:

How to Keep the Pastor Happy and Effective Or: The Care and Feeding of Shepherds

Each time a pastor stands before his congregation he stands there not as "Rev", or Pastor Pete or Pastor Johnson. This is true whether in the pulpit, at a church business meeting, in your living room or in the church office. He is there as one called by God, ordained by the larger church body, the denomination, and called by that congregation to be its spiritual shepherd.

The authority of a pastor can be compared to a policeman directing traffic. There is nothing magical in that policeman that makes it possible for him to put out his hand and traffic stops, or to wave his hand and traffic moves on. Neither is there any magical power in that badge he wears. However there is behind him the authority placed on him by the city and all its residents. By that authority he can by the simple movement of his hands cause cars to stop and go. Apart from that authority on the street corner he is a husband and father. He is someone's neighbor and a citizen of the community equal to all the others.

As a pastor shepherds his flock with an authority greater than himself, he is at the same time, and all the time, human, terribly human. Believe me, it is a fearful position to be in.

Pastors are usually reluctant to talk about matters that pertain to their own position in the church. There is the fear of sounding as if they are putting themselves on a pedestal. In 40 plus years of pastoral ministry I have sat in hundreds of business meetings and board meetings, have dealt with church problems of which some have been quite serious, have seen individuals grow in their relationship with the Lord, and seen congregations grow in their common faith and commitment, Therefore I feel I can speak on the announced topic. I speak not for my own sake, but for the sake of pastors who are to come. A clearer understanding of these matters on the part of both lay and clergy is terribly important to the health and growth of the church. There is a real need for churches to understand how to care for their pastor. Not to talk about it means that the Holy Scriptures are being neglected. Therefore this topic must be included in the preaching and teaching in the church. Anything we can do, pastor and congregation, to make and to keep that relationship harmonious must be done. If the conference superintendent doesn't have time to come to a church and give a sermon on this topic, the pastor must do it himself.

I have just completed three sermons on spiritual maturity as seen in Philippians. We saw the example of the Apostle Paul. We looked at our spiritual maturity in relationship to fellow Christians. Last Sunday it was our spiritual maturity in relationship to Christ. Today we continue in this vein as we look into spiritual maturity in relationship with your spiritual leader.

The three main points of this sermon are by no means a claim to be saying it all. In each point I will briefly present the Biblical teaching and follow that with some practical instruction.

I. Respect your Spiritual Leader as one Called by God

I speak to you as one who has served many years in pastoral ministry and who has sat with pastors, listened to them on the phone and read their letters as they opened their hearts. Bear in mind, as you prepare for your next pastor, and as you look into the future of this congregation, there is no one who is more susceptible and more sensitive to criticism than a pastor. There is no one more in need of support and encouragement, and no one more responsive to that support and encouragement than a pastor.

I Thessalonians 5:12, 13, "Now we ask you, brothers, to respect those who work hard among you, who are over you in the Lord and who admonish you. Hold them in the highest regard in love because of their work. Live in peace with each other."

Then there is I Corinthians 16:15b, 16, where the Holy Spirit speaks through Paul of those who have devoted themselves to serving the saints. "I urge you brothers to submit to such as these and to everyone who joins in the work, and labors at it."

It is understood that a pastor has a Divine call and that he would not be in pastoral ministry without it. I believe it was the great evangelist, D. L. Moody, who advised young people to not enter the pastoral ministry "unless you just can't help it." A former conference superintendent said to a gathering of pastors, as mentioned previously, "You are called of God to be pastors. Don't ever stoop so low as to be president of the United States even if you have the chance."

When you read Galatians, you realize that that church received the Apostle Paul as they would receive Christ.

In Philippians 2:12, 13 Paul had the gall to expect obedience from his flock. He felt that he had not only the right, but also the duty to expect that. Without it, how could he lead? He expected it not because he was Paul, but because he had a calling by which he was set apart by God.

In I Corinthians 4:16 and again in 7:7 and 11:1 Paul wishes everyone was just like him. He did not apologize for expecting that, nor was he embarrassed for saying it, because it was not for his own sake that he was saying it. He was saying it for the sake of his Divine call and for the good of the church.

In Philippians 3:7 Paul has the gall to ask that the flock imitate him. The writer to the Hebrews in 13:7 pleads that the readers imitate the faith of their spiritual leaders. Reading passages like that draw spiritual leaders to their knees in humility and Godly fear.

How can Paul be so bold as to say things like that? Do we believe in the Divine inspiration of Scripture? Sure we do. You see, Paul is writing as the Holy Spirit gives direction: "This is the Word of the Lord that I am giving you." That is how a good pastor leads and preaches.

Pastors are often called shepherds. That term has to do with leading sheep. I learned a lot about sheep while guarding sheep as a boy. Sheep are not herded. They are led. Our flock followed this young shepherd boy. If any sheep wandered away from the flock it was my job to bring it back within the safety of the flock. Sometimes another sheep would do that.

There are certain key members of the flock that if you get them to follow the shepherd, then you have the entire flock with you. Those sheep have a much greater effect on the flock than they realize. I guess I am talking about the church, am I not?

The entire flock can easily go astray because of one member of the flock who might decide to go off on his own or to wander. An outside happening or an untrained dog can spook the flock and suddenly they forget who the shepherd is so they scatter. When they scatter, they lose their sense of unity and their sense of direction. That makes them fearful. They expect the worst. The Shepherd then spends untold hours correcting what an outsider or a spooked insider did in just a short while.

Practical Instruction:

The congregation needs to see the pastor as a servant, not as employed by and working for the congregation or taking orders from the congregation. His relationship to the congregation is that of a physician to his patients. The best for his patients is on his heart, but he does not take his orders from them, nor does he take orders, as regards his patients, from the Hospital Board.

The pastor needs to be seen as one trained and experienced in pastoral ministry. Those trained in other fields and are looked upon as people who know their business. Even if there is another in the church who is trained and experienced in pastoral ministry, the pastor is still *the* pastor by virtue of the call the church has given him. He might not be doing things the way someone else thinks it should be done, or he might not be giving priority to the jobs that someone else thinks he should, but he is still the pastor and must be trusted to do his job; to fulfill his calling.

II. Love your Leader as one Called by the Church.

Your spiritual leader is not only called by God, but when trained and proven to be qualified he is called by the denomination and given ordination. An ordination given by the denomination is recognized and honored by many other Christian denominations. To receive ordination in our denomination there are steps that need to be followed.

There must be three years of seminary training in our denominational seminary plus a year of internship. This comes after a four-year college degree. A graduate from another seminary must have several hours of orientation in our seminary for ordination. He then must have three years of active ministry before he can apply for ordination. After application, he writes an ordination paper covering all facets of life, faith, theology and church work. There must be a recommendation from his church, an interview with the Conference Board of Ministry who recommends him to the Denominational Board of Ministry. After that interview, he is recommended to the national ministerium of the denomination. Then delegates from all the churches in North America will vote on the recommendation that comes from the national ministerium. The ordination service takes place there. Since most of you have never had the opportunity to be present at an ordination service I will share with you a part of that service.

"Address to the Ordinands": "Having been called to the ordained ministry of the church, you will now have that call confirmed by prayer and the laying on of hands. God has called you through the church to serve Jesus Christ in a special way. You have prepared and equipped yourselves for this high calling and have proved by life and work that you are qualified to be true ministers of the Word and shepherds of the flock. We, the church, pledge you our prayers and support, our fellowship and cooperation, that we may walk together in all the ways of the Lord. You have heard the Word of God concerning this holy calling. You know who we are and what we believe, and you understand the work to which you have been called. I now ask you in the presence of God and this company of people to make your confession of faith. Your solemn promises constitute your ordination vows." (Quoted with permission from "The Covenant Book of Worship", Covenant Press, 1981)

Then there are a number of questions concerning faith, doctrine, relationship with the Lord and loyalty to the church. Having already answered all these they can all publicly answer "I do". Finally there is the "Declaration of Ordination". "In the name of the Lord Jesus Christ, head of the church, and by the authority of (the denomination), I now declare you duly ordained to the office of the ministry, committing to you the authority to preach the Word, administer the sacraments, and bear rule in the church. Glory be to the Father, and to the Son, and to the Holy Spirit. Amen"

Ordination, then, is for life. However, if an ordained one is unfaithful he can be defrocked. Defrocking is done by the denominational annual meeting on the recommendation by the ministerium who at the same time will be compassionate to the defrocked brother and yet very strict with their brothers regarding ministry and conduct.

In Philippians 4:10 the Apostle Paul praises the people who cared for him. "I rejoice greatly in the Lord that at last you have renewed your concern for me. Indeed, you have been concerned . . ." Then in verse 14 he praises them that they helped him in his troubles, "Yet it was good of you to share in my troubles."

Now understand that ordination vows are a two way promise. The shepherd pledges love and loyalty to the flock and the flock pledges love and loyalty to the shepherd. Even if you were not personally present at that ordination service, you made your vows through your delegates who were there on your behalf.

Our Executive Secretary of Publications, in speaking to the delegates at the annual meeting of a conference in which I was serving said, as I repeat those words for emphasis, "If you don't like your pastor, it says more about you than it says about him". I add to that that it also works the other way. If the pastor does not like his people, it says more about him than it says about his people.

I make no claim that pastors are always correct. There are times when they, too, need advice and correction, but when a pastor is criticized, whether justly or unjustly, if that criticism is not dealt with properly, here is what happens:

1. The Holy Spirit removes his power. Scripture clearly condemns criticism of the Lord's anointed. In spite of all the trouble king Saul gave David, we see in I Samuel 24:6 that David would not make trouble for God's anointed. II Samuel 1:14 and 19:21 proclaim that there will be death for those who kill God's chosen or who even curse them. Now think about it, there is a death worse than the death of the body. That is the mental and emotional destruction and the destroying of the will that a person can inflict on another.

   Psalm 105:15 and I Chronicles 16:22 state, "Do not touch my anointed ones, do my prophets no harm." That harm can be emotional harm, which is worse than any physical harm. If God's chosen servants are unfaithful God will take care of that and his vengeance is much more effective.

2. The position of the spiritual leader of the congregation becomes negated and ineffective.

3. It destroys the spirit and the mood of the congregation.

- 119 -

4. The members of the congregation begin to have doubts about their pastor.

5. The pastor is overlooked in the making of plans and in the setting of goals.

6. The pastor responds in one or more of three ways: with anger, frustration (ulcers) or with an "I give up" attitude.

Practical Instruction:

Is there any complaint or criticism of the pastor and you feel you must talk about it, talk only with him. Maybe there is a weakness or a neglect of which he is not aware and can be easily corrected. Maybe there is a weakness of which he is aware and there is a good reason for it. Maybe he is spiritually or emotionally down and just need someone to give him love and support.

If you get no satisfaction out of going directly to the pastor, even though I am certain that you will, then, if you feel that you must take it further, speak to the chairman of the Pastoral Relations committee and no one else. Let that committee take proper steps.

By all means, follow the steps prescribed in Matthew 18:15-17. Much of the troubles people have in relationship, whether with Christian or with unbelievers, come because the teaching of Jesus in that passage is followed in reverse.

Once you have brought the matter before the PRC, if it must go that far, then drop the matter there and forget it. To talk about this matter with others in the church is absolutely forbidden because anything negative spreads like cancer in the body. To talk about it to anyone outside of your own congregation is an even more serious sin.

III. Support Your Spiritual Leader as One Called to Serve

Your pastor is called by God, ordained by the church, then called, *not hired, but called*, by the local congregation. As a pastor is installed in a church, a service led by the conference superintendent, the congregation is asked to make promises, promises that must not be taken glibly or forgotten before you get to the dinner table:

Charge to the Congregation: "Dear friends in Christ, guided by the Holy Spirit you have called (John Doe) to be your pastor. By this act you have indicated your confidence in him to be the shepherd of this parish. I charge you to receive the Word of God through him in all meekness and love. Undergird him with your prayers, assist and encourage him in the labors which will be his in the service of God. Remember always that he is God's servant and that you as God's servants are to supply his/her needs in a way that will be pleasing to God and an honor to your congregation. In all things show him your love; esteem him highly for his calling as your pastor and accept him as your spiritual leader.

"If these are your intentions, please support him and the continuing ministry of this church by standing and responding and responding to the following questions:

"Will you receive (John Doe) to be your pastor, recognizing his place in spiritual leadership and receiving the Word of God through him? If this is your promise, answer 'I will'

"Will you do your full part to supply his needs in a way that will be pleasing to God and will encourage him and share with him in the work of Christ in this church? If this is your promise, answer 'I will'." (Quoted with permission from "The Covenant Book of Worship", Covenant Press, 1981)

I give you three important ways based on Scripture of supporting your pastor:

1. Financial support. This is not salary as in payment for services rendered. It is financial support from the congregation so he can give all his time to serving the Lord and the congregation. The reason for this financial support is in numerous Scripture passages, especially I Corinthians 9:1-14. The personal touch back of it is in Philippians 4:17, "Not that I am looking for a gift, but I am looking for what may be credited to your account". Note that the financial support is not only for the pastor's sake, but for the sake of the church as well.

Sometimes a pastor will decline an increase in financial support in order to ease the pressure on the budget. To do so is a disservice to the church and to pastors who will follow him.

Sometimes a church holds back on the financial support given to the pastor so they can give more to missions, repair the church building or put up a new one. That means you are forcing the pastor to support the missionaries or pay for a major part of the new building.

2. Through words of encouragement. A simple "Thank you" goes a mighty long way.

The most important thing any of us can do for another, whoever that might be, is to help that other person feel good about himself. If your compliments happen to go to his head, that's his problem. He will have to deal with the consequences of that. You did your part.

Have you ever thought of this? A pastor can go weeks or even months and see no visible or tangible result of his efforts. A carpenter can stand back and see the result of his efforts. A farmer can see his crop come up and grow to harvest in the bins. An office worker can see a stack of paper that was done that day. A pastor might go weeks without seeing a soul saved and when a soul is saved it is not a tangible or visible result in the human sense.

A pastor needs a hobby so he can make something to hold in his hands. There is something about a tangible object held in the hand of the craftsman of which he can say "I did this", or a fish in the bucket or maybe even a golf score card stuck on the refrigerator.

3. <u>Pray for your pastor:</u> The Apostle Paul often exhorted his people to pray for him. If the Apostle Paul needed prayer that much, how much more do all the rest of God's pastors and missionaries need prayer. I have heard pastors say, "When the people are praying for me I know it."

Practical Instruction:

I repeat, the monthly check that your church gives the pastor is not payment for services rendered. How do you put a monetary value on that kind of work? In the Old Testament the support of priests was opposed to such thinking as is also the teaching of the New Testament on the support of missionaries and pastors. That monthly check to the pastor from the church , in the Scriptural sense, is the support the church gives so he can give full time to being the spiritual shepherd of the church.

In the Old Testament the purpose of the tithe was to give support to the priests, the spiritual leaders. Other matters, such as the care of the temple and its expenses, were taken care of through the free will offerings. The New Testament application of this means that our tithes are for the support of the pastors and missionaries. Building expenses, utilities, etc. come out of the free will offering above the tithe. You have not given a free will offering until the tithe is taken care of.

Be an encourager. Be a friend. Very often the loneliest person in the church is the pastor. Be a pray-er. That cannot be emphasized too much. Pray for your pastor. Pray for your church, its leaders, boards and committees. Pray for your fellow church members, one by one and by name.

I took a retired pastor with me to visit a new pastor recently moved into our district. Upon entering the home of this pastor the retired pastor took the new pastor's hand and said, "I pray for you every day because in this place you sure need it." That pretty well says it. No matter who the pastor is or what the church is, "In this place you sure need it." Without his touch with God, what happens to a pastor's ministry? Without the prayers of his parishioners, what happens to his touch with God?

Conclusion:

I have been pretty straightforward with you today. Whatever comes of this message will depend on the spirit in which you receive it. In being straightforward I have wanted very much to be thorough while also honest, loving and tactful. I have not succeeded in being thorough. There is so much more to be said. I sincerely hope I succeeded in being loving and tactful. May the Lord bless each of you as you seek to be the best servant of the Lord that you can be.

Points to Ponder

Go back over the "Practical Instruction" sections in this chapter. In each section ask yourself/yourselves how these instructions are working in your church and what can be done to apply them or to apply them more firmly.

CHAPTER 11:

Growing Churches

There are many conditions and circumstances that contribute to the growth of a church, but according to those who have studied the question of what makes a church grow, a condition that is very often present is this: the pastor has been there at least 20 years. There you have another reason to keep your pastor emotionally and physically healthy and happy. Those who stay that long have had a good relationship with a supportive congregation who is generous with encouragement. I know a pastor who was told by his church to leave. He went to another church and at this point has been in that church more than 20 years. Perhaps that says something about where the problem was. The way church members treat their pastor or do not treat their pastor (even silence says a lot) is a good indicator of the growth or lack of growth in a church. It appears that whenever a church gets a new pastor it is at that point that a few people leave the church.

I have heard it said more than a couple times that it is healthy for a church to change pastor every few years. A change of voice in the pulpit and a change of emphasis will draw interest and help the people to grow more solid in their faith they say. I find that interesting. My children sat under the same pastor for the first 18 years of their lives. They all turned into solid Christians and exemplary people. How about my wife who sat under the same ministry for 43 years and is a good example of a healthy, full of faith Christian?

Consider, now, those times when your church was seeking a pastor. A candidate for the pastorate came to preach a sermon and meet with the Search Committee. Then he was on his way. You now have your congregational meeting where you talk about the candidate. People share their observations and some talk about what they had heard about this candidate. It is usually the best attended business meeting of the church. Of the voters present, there will be those who had not darkened the door of the church in many months. There will be those nominal members who are not much interested in the work of the church but are there to warm their place in a pew on Sunday mornings. Prayer meetings and Bible Studies are not in their schedule. But, of course, there will be those who have done their homework, know whereof they speak and truly seek to follow the will of the Lord.

I ask you, who is willing to submit himself to that kind of meeting while not being present? Like it or not, pastors are called upon to submit themselves and their families to just that very thing. I spoke with a young man, himself a pastor's son, about this thing of placing self and family wide open before a group of people, some positive and interested and some the other extreme, those who are deliberately looking for something negative of which to speak. That young man said. That is exactly why I did not enter the ministry". However, God did not relinquish the call. Later this young man did enter the pastoral ministry.

Chapter 12:

Pastor to Pastors

What can I say that would be good for a pastor? Maybe after all those years of pastoral ministry and many more years of prayer and meditation I do have something that might be good for you, even though probably nothing new.

In my writings, I have not intended to place you on a pedestal and, by all means, do not think of yourself in that way. It is, however, important that you be the kind of person in the church and in the community that people will look up to and respect. I am sure you have noticed that what I have written about the layperson's responsibility to the pastor also works the other way. Work and pray to become one who has love and respect for every member of his flock.

To whom does a pastor turn for help? Really, there is no one. Every pastor needs a mentor. The best thing for a pastor is to have another pastor with whom he can sit down, "let his hair down", and bare his heart and soul. The mentor will be a confidant who will keep names and experiences hidden in his heart and mind (I have had many experiences and conversations that my wife knows nothing about. She does not want to know so she can meet these people on Sunday morning with nothing in her mind to interfere with a good relationship). Pastor and pastor can cry together and they can give each other encouragement. They can offer suggestions and maybe even advice. Who else is there? If your mentor, or even yourself, are not willing to be phoned or called out at 2 a.m. you will not be good mentors.

Pastors, consider the hearts of the people in the pew. Picture yourself in each person's special place and ask yourself how that person will receive what you are saying. How about during the week, going to the sanctuary and sit in various places in the pews. Think of the person who usually sits there. Put yourself in his days if you possibly can. What is his life like? What does he need? What can you say that would give him a lift for the week? Do this often. Sitting in the pew is not the same as standing in the pulpit, you know.

As I had begun to make some progress at recovery from my bad experiences I sat in the pew one Sunday and listened to a pastor tell his congregation to turn all the troubles over to the Lord. It was a good sermon and it was done pretty much the way I would have done it at one time, but now, as I sat in the pew, the words that kept working in my mind were, "That's easy for you to say". So how would I do it now? I would leave the platform and come down among the people and speak heart to heart. Even pray with those who ask for a prayer. I would invite those who wish to come to my office where we could talk some more and pray. Maybe I would even have to call in someone who has the gift of exorcism. Standing in the pulpit and dropping the Word down on people is not the end of preaching.

I think of all the times I have said to my people, "Turn it over to the Lord. He loves you"; 'The Lord forgives you"; "He will carry your burden". Now I look back and hear them saying, "That's easy for you to say. Now tell me how." and "I agree, but how can I turn it over to the Lord?" "How can I let go? Those burdens keep hanging on", "How can the Lord love me?" and "I don't feel forgiven."

God will bless you, dear brother pastors. May He give you a spirit to love your people. May He give you a congregation who stands behind you and with you.

Pastors, when you hear rumors of a brother pastor being in trouble in a church, do not be quick to believe what you hear and do not write him off. Do something. Hear his story. He needs you to be a Barnabas. On a vacation trip, we stopped to see a pastor whom we had heard was not well. One thing he said has stuck with me, "People keep giving me Bible verses and telling me that the Lord will lift you above your earthly problems. That's not my problem. There's nothing wrong with my relationship with the Lord. My faith is fine. The problem is; I have pain."

Don't let your walk with the Lord become commonplace. Advice I often give to young pastors is this, "Don't let your Bible become mainly a book of sermon texts". I felt so sorry for a teenage boy in Colorado. We pulled into a filling station. I got out of the car and stood there looking up at the mountains. This boy came out and asked, "What are you looking at?" I said, "I am looking at the mountains. They're beautiful." Said the boy, "O, those. I don't even notice them anymore. I see them every day." My thought was, "You better wake up, son.

Notice the beauty in life. Don't let it become so common that it is missed". That is my advice to all Christians. Jesus can be fresh every morning. (Lamentations 3:22, 23)

A seminary friend was feeling very low. He went to talk with the Dean about it. That meeting concluded with the Dean saying, "Come with me. I have a friend with whom I want you to have a visit." The student was led to the chapel where he was told to sit down in front of a large painting of Sallman's "Head of Christ". "Sit here and talk with Him a while" were the instructions as the Dean walked out and left the student there.

A good thought for all of us: And as we talk with our Lord, perhaps we need to talk less and listen more.

I wish to say a word of appreciation to those superintendents who made an effort to be of help, but generally speaking, I did not find help in Superintendents. One superintendent I worked with through the years could definitely be called an encourager or a mentor to pastors. Another was a good listener when I went to his office to open my heart. He then phoned a couple weeks later to see how I was doing. That was much appreciated. Another was known for making the rounds and visiting every pastor in the conference on a regular basis. His visits, which were very much appreciated, went something like this: he would arrive unannounced at my office. After my "Good to see you", he would ask, "How are your problems?" a standard question of his. About the time I opened my mouth to tell him about my problems, he was again on his way

You, the conference superintendents are the pastor's pastor. You are often the only person in flesh and bones to whom a pastor can turn. (I have often asked myself, "To whom do the Superintendents go?). Your most important job is to keep the pastors happy. Even if that commandeers the majority of your time, it could well be the best thing you could do to strengthen your Conference and see your churches grow.

I propose that every Conference have a cadre of people available to help depressed and troubled pastors. This cadre could consist of retired pastors to whom other pastors can turn for someone to listen, encourage and maybe give suggestions and advice, but someone to listen to another as he unburdens his heart could be the most important part of such a ministry. Also, surely somewhere in the Conference there are Christian, professional counselors and psychologists who would be willing to give some time to building the Conference by strengthening the pastors who have such a need. It would be a wonderful contribution on the part of such a professional. Any cost would be worthy ministry by the conference.

After retiring, I attended a pastors' conference. At one of the small group meetings of 20 to 30 pastors the leader spoke of the pastor as a leader who can take the church where he wants it to go while the congregation works with him. I know very well what that is. I had done that, but now, with that awful experience at church "G" still hanging on in my memory I asked, "What do you do when the congregation refuses to follow?" I guess he, too, had heard about my reputation, because with a stern look on his face and pointing a finger right at me he said, "It's up to you to see that they follow". I said no more as these words burned in my heart. My thought was "You have no idea where I have been and you do not know some of the people whom I was sent to lead". It was the worst conference I have ever attended. Conference Superintendents, please do your best to understand your pastors and the situations they are in. Pastors, please do your best to understand each other.

When I left church "E" and again at church "G" the conference superintendent said that he would move me out and then come in and work on the problem. May I say two things about that? (1) If you say that, then do it and do it soon. (2) Would it not be better to come in and work on the problem while the pastor is still there? Moving the pastor is the easy and temporary way out. To move him out before facing the problem is to say that you, too, see him as the problem. When troubles arose at church "E", I learned from three or four knowledgeable sources that this had been going on for many years. The pastor leaves, a new pastor comes and the situation settles down for a while only to rise up again.

One further thought to Conference Superintendents: Avoid putting pastors in pigeonholes. For example, do not label a pastor as a small town or small church pastor with no opportunity to move to something different as he grows and changes through his experiences, personally and spiritually. "Also, do not label him as a 'trouble maker' or as a 'less than good choice'. One or two bad experiences does not tell you that."

A Supplemental Thought

Upon retirement I was blessed to renew friendship with a teacher I had known in my high school years. She was now over 90 years old but was very active physically and alert mentally. She was also very much alive spiritually. This lady was known for her generosity with compliments. Some felt that she was so generous with compliments that they lost their meaning. She must have been aware of that too because she would often, after giving a compliment add, "I mean it".

She died at the age of 98 and in the absence of the pastor I was honored to conduct her funeral. A relative showed me her Bible. It doubled as a file cabinet, being loaded with clippings. The margins of her Bible were literally covered with notations and short quotes. The following poem was taped inside the front cover of her Bible.

I KNOW SOMETHING GOOD ABOUT YOU

Wouldn't this old world be better
        If the folks you meet would say –
"I know something good about you!"
        And treat us just that way?

Wouldn't it be fine and dandy
        If each hand clasp, fond and true,
Carried with it this assurance –
        "I know something good about you!"

Wouldn't life be lots more happy
        If the good that's in us all
Were the only things about us
        That folks bothered to recall?

Wouldn't life be lots more happy
        If we praised the good we see?
For there's such a lot of goodness
        In the worst of you and me

Wouldn't it be nice to practice
        That fine way of thinking, too?
You know something good about me,
        I know something good about you?

Author Unknown